Edmund Clowney is this generation's
ical preaching. For decades he was the \
encourage evangelical preachers to make Christ the focus of all their
messages, since he is the aim of all the Scriptures. Now, many others
have joined Clowney's gospel chorus, but none with greater mastery
than he of the harmonies that weave the symphony of grace throughout the Bible. As Clowney shares with us the jewels of his research,
message, and heart, we discern ever more clearly how to make the Pearl
of Great Price shine through all the treasures of Scripture.

> —BRYAN CHAPELL
> President and Professor of Practical Theology
> Covenant Seminary

Edmund Clowney has given a wonderful gift to the church in general
and to preachers in particular. *Preaching Christ in All of Scripture* is the
kind of book that isn't just about preaching. It's about Christ and the
call on all believers to see him and his glory in all of God's Word.
Preachers can rejoice and profit from the practical and profound teaching, and all believers can rejoice in the awesome reality of Jesus as Lord.

> —STEPHEN W. BROWN
> Professor of Preaching
> Reformed Theological Seminary

Here is instruction from a master Bible teacher on how to preach God-
honoring, Christ-centered, Spirit-empowered sermons. Edmund
Clowney's classes at Westminster Seminary transformed my understanding of how the whole Bible fits together, and I expect this book
will do the same for all who read it.

> —WAYNE GRUDEM
> Research Professor of Bible and Theology
> Phoenix Seminary

Ed Clowney taught me how to preach the gospel to postmodern people. To anyone who wants to learn how to do so as well, these sermons are priceless.

—TIM KELLER
Senior Pastor
Redeemer Presbyterian Church of New York City

Christians must learn again to read the whole Bible as a testimony to Jesus Christ. Dr. Edmund Clowney shows the way to a truly Christian interpretation of the Bible in *Preaching Christ in All of Scripture*. This book is urgently needed in today's church, for too many preachers seem to be at a loss in dealing with the Old Testament. Dr. Clowney shows us how the Old Testament reveals Christ in its great themes and in its rich details. Edmund Clowney is one of the great Christian leaders and pastoral theologians of our time. Do not miss this book.

—R. ALBERT MOHLER, JR., PRESIDENT
The Southern Baptist Theological Seminary

PREACHING CHRIST
IN ALL OF SCRIPTURE

PREACHING CHRIST IN ALL OF SCRIPTURE

EDMUND P. CLOWNEY

CROSSWAY BOOKS
WHEATON, ILLINOIS

Preaching Christ in All of Scripture

Copyright © 2003 by Edmund P. Clowney

Published by Crossway Books,
a publishing ministry of Good News Publishers,
1300 Crescent Street,
Wheaton, Illinois 60187

Cover design: Josh Dennis

Cover photo: David Alan Wolters

First printing 2003

Printed in the United States of America

Library of Congress Cataloging-in-Publication Data
Clowney, Edmund P.
    Preaching Christ in all of Scripture / Edmund P. Clowney.
        p. cm.
    Includes bibliographical references and index.
    ISBN 13: 978-1-58134-452-3 (tpb. : alk. paper)
    ISBN 10: 1-58134-452-X
    1. Jesus Christ—Person and offices—Sermons. 2. Bible—Sermons.
3. Sermons, American. 4. Reformed Church—Sermons. 5. Bible—
Homiletical use. 6. Preaching. I. Title.
BT203.C57   2003
251—dc21   2002154807

VP		17	16	15	14	13	12	11	10	
15	14	13	12	11	10	9	8	7	6	5

CONTENTS

PREFACE

BIBLE READERS AND TEACHERS know that the Bible is a storybook. My Sunday school teacher in the primary department recommended the Bible to me, and I began to read it. At a crisis in my college days I knew that my one hope was to read the Bible. I read it, not in snatches, but in hours and days out of desperation. I started in Genesis chapter 1. When I reached the book of Jonah, I came upon the verse, "Salvation is of the Lord!" I realized then that the Bible did not give a full history of Israel, but a history of God's work of saving his chosen people. It is all about what God did. He who holds the worlds in his hand came down to save us. The Bible is the story of how God came down to be born of the Virgin Mary, to live and die for us, and to rise in triumph from the tomb. It was not my grip on God that was my hope, but his grip on me.

As I continued to study and teach the Bible, I saw increasingly that God's promise in the Old Testament was kept in the New Testament. It was kept in the coming of God the Son. John's Gospel witnesses to the deity of Jesus Christ, the Word made flesh. Jesus, John tells us, is the one whom Isaiah saw in his vision of God seated on his throne between the cherubim (John 12:41).

The Angel who appeared to Moses at the burning bush in the desert identified himself as the "I AM" God. Not only do the four Gospels tell the story of Jesus. So do the five books of Moses, who gave God's promise of the Prophet to come. So does the rest of the Old Testament. Remember that the apostle Paul, preaching in every synagogue from the Scriptures, was preaching from the scrolls of the Old Testament. Paul gave the apostolic witness to Jesus in whom all the Old Testament Scripture is fulfilled.

Preachers who ignore the history of redemption in their preaching are ignoring the witness of the Holy Spirit to Jesus in all the
Scriptures.

This book begins with two chapters, then adds more than a
dozen sermons that reflect the united witness of the Old and New
Testaments to Christ. Chapter 1 seeks to show that Christ is presented in the whole Old Testament. Chapter 2 offers help in
"Preparing a Sermon That Presents Christ." The sermons that follow
are given as examples of messages showing how particular texts, seen
in their context, do present Christ. Other Bible passages alluded to
in the sermons are not referenced, unless quoted. The sermons are
offered as messages to be heard as preaching, not as footnoted theses
for study.

I do pray that readers may be encouraged to turn to the Scriptures
and know for themselves the joy of hearing Jesus, as they travel with
him to Emmaus on Easter Morning.

—Edmund P. Clowney

1

CHRIST IN ALL OF SCRIPTURE

PREACHING CHRIST FROM the Old Testament means that we preach, not synagogue sermons, but sermons that take account of the full drama of redemption, and its realization in Christ. To see the text in relation to Christ is to see it in its larger context, the context of God's purpose in revelation. We do not ignore the specific message of the text, nor will it do to write an all-purpose Christocentric sermon finale and tag it for weekly use.

You must preach Christ as the text presents him. If you are tempted to think that most Old Testament texts do not present Christ, reflect on both the unity of Scripture and the fullness of Jesus Christ. Christ is present in the Bible as the Lord and as the Servant.

CHRIST THE LORD OF THE COVENANT

The New Testament applies the title *kurios* (Lord) to Christ (e.g., Heb. 1:10; 1 Pet. 3:15). That Greek term, used in the Septuagint version of the Old Testament to translate "Yahweh," became the short designation of the Lord Jesus Christ. Both the Old Testament and the New also use the term "Lord" to designate "the God and Father of our Lord Jesus Christ," as in Peter's quotation of Psalm 2 in Acts 4:26 (NKJV):

> The kings of the earth took their stand,
> And the rulers were gathered together
> Against the LORD and against His Christ.

Most of the designations of God in the Old Testament refer to the living God with no distinction of the persons of the Trinity. But the Second Person of the Trinity appears as the "Lord" in many passages. John's Gospel shows that this is the case when John quotes Isaiah 6:10 and adds, "These things said Isaiah, because he saw his glory; and he spake of him" (John 12:41, ASV). Since the quotation is from Isaiah's vision of God's glory in the temple, it is clear that John views that glory of the Lord enthroned as the glory of Christ, the Logos.

Paul does the same in Ephesians 4:8 when he quotes from Psalm 68:18 (NKJV), applying to Christ's ascension words spoken of the Lord's exaltation:

When He ascended on high,
He led captivity captive,
And gave gifts to men.

The living God revealed in the Old Testament is the triune God. To be sure, the Incarnation brought to light Old Testament teaching that had still been in shadow. Yet the Angel of the Lord's presence did reveal the mystery of the One who could be both distinguished from God and identified with him. When the Commander of the Army of the Lord confronted Joshua in front of Jericho with a drawn sword, he told him to take off his sandals, because he was on holy ground. The Commander revealed himself to Joshua as the Lord himself (Josh. 5:13–6:5). The Lord God had given that same warning when he called to Moses from the flaming bush. The Angel of the Lord spoke to Moses from the bush, but identified himself as I AM, the God of the fathers. This is a well-established pattern in the theophanies of the Old Testament. The Angel was, in fact, God the Son, the Lord. He is the Angel of God's presence who spoke with Abraham (Gen. 18:1-2, 22, 33), who wrestled with Jacob (Genesis 32), who went before Israel (Ex. 23:20), whom Moses desired to know (Ex. 33:12-13), and who appeared to Manoah to announce the birth of Samson (Judges 13). The Angel speaks as Lord, bears the name of

God, and reveals the glory of God (Ex. 23:21). Glimpsing his face in the early dawn, Jacob says he has seen the face of God (Gen. 32:30).

Anthony T. Hanson has argued that "the central affirmation [of the New Testament writers] is that the preexistent Jesus was present in much of Old Testament history, and that therefore it is not a question of tracing types in the Old Testament for New Testament events, but rather of tracing the activity of the same Jesus in the old and new dispensations."[1]

To support his thesis, Hanson examines Pauline references, the book of Hebrews, Stephen's speech in Acts, the Fourth Gospel, and the Catholic Epistles. He examines Paul's account in 1 Corinthians 10:1-11 of the experiences of Israel under Moses. Hanson then appeals to the Greek Old Testament, the Septuagint, to note the use of *kurios* in Exodus 14. *Kurios* or *ho kurios* is used throughout the chapter, while *theos* (God) appears in verses 19 and 31. Hanson finds that such verses support Paul's distinguishing God from Christ the Lord in this chapter. He holds that Paul read "Christ" wherever *kurios* appears in the Septuagint passage. Christ was the Lord who delivered Israel from Egypt. As the Angel of God in the pillar of cloud, the Lord guided and guarded the Israelites in the Exodus. He led them from ahead, then went behind them to remain there through the night. There he screened them from the pursuing Egyptians (Ex. 14:19):

> And Israel saw the mighty hand, the things that *kurios* did to the Egyptians; and the people feared *kurios,* and they believed God and Moses his servant (Ex. 14:31, literal translation).

The cloud of which Paul speaks (1 Cor. 10:1) is the cloud of Exodus 14, but it is worthy of note that in the Septuagint of Exodus 13:21 it is God (*theos*) who "led them, in the day by the pillar of cloud, to show them the way, and in the night by a pillar of fire."[2] (In Hebrew, the name of God is "Yahweh" in this passage.)

---

[1] Anthony Tyrrell Hanson, *Jesus Christ in the Old Testament* (London: SPCK, 1965), 172.
[2] The Septuagint Version of the Old Testament (London: Bagster & Sons; New York: Harper, n.d.).

Pressing the point that Paul thought "Christ" where he read *kurios* in the account of the Exodus, Hanson so interprets 1 Corinthians 10:9, "Nor let us tempt Christ, as some of them also tempted, and were destroyed by serpents" (NKJV). Paul, he holds, simply identified the Lord who led Israel through the wilderness as the Lord Christ.

In 1 Corinthians 10:9 the reading *Christon* (with the weight of the Chester Beatty papyrus) may be preferred to *kurion* (Sinaiticus, Vaticanus). On either reading, Hanson appears to be correct in claiming that Paul is thinking of Christ as the Lord who delivered Israel from Egypt, leading them through his presence manifested in the Angel.

Hanson refers to an important comment by C. H. Dodd on Romans 10:12-13: "Wherever the term *Kyrios,* Lord, is applied to Jehovah in the OT, Paul seems to hold that it points forward to the coming revelation of God in the Lord Jesus Christ."[3] Hanson holds that this statement is "at once too sweeping and too tame." Too sweeping, because Paul does not always refer *kurios* in the Greek Old Testament to Christ (e.g., Rom. 9:28; 11:3).[4] Too tame, because in Paul's view *kurios* does not simply point forward to Christ, but names Christ, present as Lord.

We may not be convinced of all the intricate exegetical reasoning that Hanson mounts to demonstrate his thesis. We may conclude that at times he stresses an identification of the Lord with Christ in Paul's thinking that is too dependent on Septuagint use, or too superficial for Paul's profound theology. Orthodox trinitarian theology took centuries seeking to unpack the distinction of persons and the unity of being (or "substance") that are implied in the way Paul worshiped the one God of his fathers in the full revelation of Father, Son, and Holy Spirit. It was easier for Paul to pass from the Father to the Son,

---

[3] C. H. Dodd (*Romans,* Moffatt New Testament Commentaries [London: Hodder & Stoughton, 1942]), quoted in Hanson, *Jesus Christ in the Old Testament,* 39.

[4] To these instances many others could be added. For example, Paul writes that "God reckoneth righteousness apart from works" (Rom. 4:6, ASV) and supports the statement with a quotation from Psalm 32:2: "Blessed is the man against whom the Lord will not count his sin" (ESV).

or from the Son to the Spirit, than it is for scholars who have tried to formulate the mystery.

Where Hanson has traced out the strong recognition of Christ as the *kurios* in Paul or Hebrews, other studies could balance the picture by demonstrating how strongly Paul's theology is centered on the Father, or by discovering Paul again as the theologian of the Holy Spirit. Yet Hanson rightly alerts us to a more New Testament understanding of the centrality of Christ in the Old Testament. Jesus Christ is one with the Lord. It was the Spirit of Christ who spoke through the prophets (1 Pet. 1:10-12). Interpreting a Septuagint passage that says to fear nothing but the name of the Lord of Hosts himself, Peter substitutes "the Christ" for "himself" (1 Pet. 3:15; Isa. 8:12-13).

Hanson, however, uses the clear presence of Christ as Lord in the Old Testament to minimize typology. He takes it to be evident that we cannot have in any particular passage both the actual presence of Christ as Lord and also a type of Christ. This may seem evident, but it ignores the richness of Old Testament revelation. A text to the point is one that Hanson discusses without taking account of the symbolism at its heart—the passage where Moses strikes the Rock at God's command (Ex. 17:1-7). There the Lord is present, standing on the rock, but the Rock itself becomes a symbol, associated with the name of God, and therefore with God the Rock in symbol (Deut. 32:4). Symbolically, the Rock represented the incarnate Christ, as Paul says (1 Cor. 10:4).

John's Gospel emphasizes the full deity of Jesus Christ as the Logos, the Word who is not only with God but is God (John 1:1). Jesus says, "Before Abraham was, I AM" (John 8:58, NKJV). John, therefore, speaks of the glory that Isaiah saw in his vision of the Lord enthroned in the temple as the glory of Christ: "Isaiah said this because he saw Jesus' glory and spoke about him" (John 12:41, NIV).

Paul affirms the deity of Christ when he writes, "For in Christ all the fullness of the Deity lives in bodily form" (Col. 2:9, NIV). The Son of God possesses all the attributes of God. He is "a Spirit, infinite, eternal, and unchangeable, in his being wisdom, power, holiness, justice, goodness and truth" (Westminster Shorter Catechism, question 4). The Second Person of the Trinity became man to be one with his creatures.

Therefore, the Lordship of Christ does not begin with his resurrection glory and ascended rule. The divine Lordship is his eternally. For that reason we do not understand the Lordship of Christ first in terms of the covenant. Rather, we understand the covenant as established by the Lord. Traditional Reformed theology has spoken of the "Covenant of Redemption." This term has been used for the covenant between the Father and the Son that established God's plan of redemption. The Father willed to send the Son into the world to redeem those given by the Father to the Son (John 17). The Son willed to come into the world and to complete the work of salvation. Jesus therefore speaks of coming from the Father and returning to the Father (John 3:13).

The promise of God's covenant is the goal of Old Testament history. It is grounded in his sure oath that the Son of God would become man to save his people from their sins. John Murray, in his conversations with me, has well pointed out that John 3:16 speaks of the giving of the *divine* Son, since that giving included the sending of the Son into the world (John 17:3-4). Paul rejoices in the order of God's eternal plan (Rom. 11:33-36). God's covenant promise to Abraham required his own coming in the person of his Son.

The history of redemption is structured by God's covenant promise and moves forward in the "seasons" of God's saving work. After the resurrection, the disciples asked Jesus, "Lord, are you at this time going to restore the kingdom to Israel?" (Acts 1:6, NIV). Jesus replied, "It is not for you to know the times or dates the Father has set by his own authority" (v. 7, NIV).

The author of Hebrews also speaks of the times in the history of God's revelation. These seasons or epochs are marked by major events in the unfolding of God's plan. The popular *Scofield Reference Bible* speaks of the periods of the history of redemption as dispensations. According to the 1917 edition of the *Scofield Bible,* the period concerned with Israel lasted from the call of Abraham to the beginning of the church in Acts 2. Dispensationalism teaches that God offers different means of salvation in the different periods. Salvation by works was the way of salvation in the period of Israel, and will be again in the millennium. The "church age" was an unforeseen interruption in the history of salvation. The four Gospels therefore are for Israel, not the church. No Old Testament prophecies predicted it. The prophetic clock stopped.

On this view, the Lord's Prayer is not given to the church, but to Israel. The *Scofield* note explains that "forgive us our debts as we forgive our debtors" cannot be a prayer given to the church, for the petition rests "on legal ground." Israel asks for forgiveness on the ground of the good work of forgiving. Scofield dispensational theology was for many years the standard evangelical theology in many churches and Bible schools. At present, leading dispensational theologians have come to realize that the Old Testament, as well as the New, teaches salvation by grace. Few scholars now follow this works/grace division between the Old Testament and the New.

On the other hand, the spread of the redemptive-historical understanding of the Scriptures in Reformed circles has brought fresh emphasis on the importance of the periods of that history. We may rejoice that the division between Reformed and dispensational theologians has been diminishing as both turn to the Scriptures.[5] Before Geerhardus Vos at Princeton Theological Seminary brought into American Calvinism the history of redemption and of revelation, classical Reformed theology used separate proof-texts to establish biblical doctrines. John Murray at Westminster Seminary in Philadelphia, however, had studied under Vos at Princeton. Murray taught a course in biblical theology. He proceeded through the periods of the history of redemption: creation to fall; fall to flood; flood to the call of Abraham; Abraham to Moses; Moses to Christ. Murray summarized the theology of each period and showed how each prepared for and pointed toward the full range of systematic theology in the New Testament.

Recent Bible commentaries, for example, the Word series,[6] use

---

[5] Lewis Sperry Chafer, the original theologian at Dallas, was a Calvinist in his theology.
[6] *Word Biblical Commentaries* (Waco, Tex.: Word, published in the 1980s and 90s).

the insights of biblical theology in their expositions. Some of these commentaries are too concessive to critical theories and the documentary hypotheses, but they provide exhaustive bibliography and condensed scholarship for biblical-theological understanding of texts.

The epochs of the history of redemption show the Lordship of the Second Person of the Trinity. It is the coming of the Lord that is the climax of the epochs of redemption. The Lord comes to possess his people. In covenantal blessing he possesses them that they may possess him. "I will walk among you and be your God, and you will be my people" (Lev. 26:12, NIV). The promise of his coming mounts like a sea-wave in Old Testament history. The Lord always takes the initiative in redemption. From the sin of Adam in the garden through the triumph of evil in the generation of the deluge, the promise remains, and is marked by the sign of the rainbow. The Lord called Noah, and swore his faithfulness to Abraham. He revealed himself to Jacob at Bethel, and came down the stairway from heaven to stand over Jacob and repeat the promise. He called Moses, and demanded that Pharaoh let his people go that they might serve him in worship. He is Lord. He delivers his people that they may be his servants. Moses declared to them the Lord's blessing if they remained faithful to him, but his curse if they rebelled. After Joshua led them into the land God had given them, the people turned aside and worshiped the Baal of the Canaanites. The Lord sent invaders in judgment but repeatedly delivered his people from those invaders, until at last he abandoned them to their idolatry. The period of the judges pointed toward Israel's need for a king. Samuel anointed Saul, then David, as king of Israel. David subdued the surrounding nations, and prepared for the building of the temple where the Lord would dwell in the midst of his people.

When Solomon dedicated the temple, he confessed that God had kept all his promises to Moses. Israel had received the peace and prosperity the Lord had promised them in the land (1 Kings 8:56). The blessings had been given. Half of the tribes recited them on Mount Gerizim. But then came the curses that had been recited on Mount Ebal (see Deut. 11:29).

CHRIST THE SERVANT OF THE COVENANT

Christ who is the Lord is also the Servant of the Lord. He is the true vine, the true Son, the true Israel. Where a righteous servant of the Lord appears in Old Testament history, it is the true Servant who is prefigured. God makes his covenant, claiming his people as his, and giving them a claim on him. "Lord" and "Servant" express that relation. The Lord's demand to Pharaoh was, "Let my people go, that they may serve me" (Ex. 10:3, ESV). Serving the Lord means worship and obedience. Jesus Christ consummates the covenant relation from both sides.

The Old Testament promises the coming of the Lord and also the coming of the Servant of the Lord. When the Lord condemns the failure of Israel's shepherds to care for the sheep, he declares that he himself will come to shepherd them (Ezek. 34:11-16). He also says that he will set up one shepherd, his servant David, over them to feed them: "I the LORD will be their God, and my servant David will be prince among them" (Ezek. 34:24, NIV).[7]

Old Testament history is prophetic history, describing covenant blessings, the covenant curse, and the wonder of God's great salvation to come in the latter days. For the "day of the LORD" to come, for God's kingdom to come, the covenant must be fulfilled from both sides. Hanson seeks to shrink typology in the New Testament by his interpretation of the terms that express it. He concludes that it was only beginning to infect the writers of the New Testament. Where it seems to have arrived, as in the sign of Jonah in Matthew's account (Matt. 12:38-41), he is ready to suggest that it originated in the early church's study of the Old Testament. He even pleads with respect to Jesus' reference to the lifting up of the serpent in the wilderness (John 3:14-15), that since no word for "type" is used, "we are left to draw the conclusion ourselves."[8]

---

[7] F. F. Bruce has traced the theme of the Shepherd King in the Old Testament, particularly in the prophecy of Zechariah. There the royal Shepherd is *geber 'ămîtî*, "the man who stands next to me" (13:7); cf. "the man of your right hand" (Ps. 80:17).

[8] Hanson notes that Barnabas Lindars points out the use of *sēmeion* with respect to the pole of Moses in the Septuagint of Numbers 21:9. He argues from the fact that no such term is used in the Gospel passage (Hanson, *Jesus Christ in the Old Testament*, 175-176; citing Barnabas Lindars, *New Testament Apologetic* [London: SCM, 1961], 266).

It is true that the New Testament does not often speak of the way it interprets the Old, and we are often left to draw our own conclusions. But the grand structure is clear. What Jesus does as the Servant of the Lord cannot be described as a mere "'parallel situation' phenomenon," a term Hanson uses to explain away the typical reference.[9] He is right in insisting that the activity of the Lord himself in the Old Testament is not merely a *type* of his activity as Lord in the New Testament. However, the actions and roles of Adam, Noah, Abraham, Isaac, Jacob, Joseph, Moses, Aaron, Joshua, David, and the rest are not to be set alongside the person and work of Jesus Christ as less effective performances of the same kind of service. Leonhard Goppelt, in his article *"typos"* in the *Theological Dictionary of the New Testament*, and in his book entitled *Typos,* has shown the distinctiveness of Paul's typology in Romans 5. It is found in Paul's eschatological focus. The coming of the Messiah does not take us back to a golden age of the past, restoring its glories. Rather, the coming of Christ brings the fulfillment, the realization of what was anticipated by God's servants, the saviors, prophets, kings, priests, and judges of the Old Covenant. Countering other views, Goppelt says, "Instead, the typological idea of the consummation of God's redemptive plan appears to be the heart of the Old Testament eschatology." He acknowledges the theme of restoration, but insists that "the typological idea of consummation of salvation is the core; the concept of restoration provides the appropriate clothing"[10] (see Sidney Greidanus, *Sola Scriptura, The Modern Preacher and the Ancient Text,* and *Preaching Christ from the Old Testament).*[11]

SYMBOLISM AND TYPOLOGY

The history of the covenant that leads to Christ also anticipates Christ in its symbolism. Symbolism has a bad name in current

---

[9] Hanson, *Jesus Christ in the Old Testament,* 175.

[10] Leonhard Goppelt, *Typos: The Typological Interpretation of the Old Testament in the New,* trans. D. H. Madvig (Grand Rapids, Mich.: Eerdmans, 1982), 28, note 99.

[11] Sidney Greidanus, *Sola Scriptura: Problems and Principles in Preaching Historical Texts* (Eugene, Ore.: Wipf & Stock, 2001); *The Modern Preacher and the Ancient Text: Interpreting and Preaching Biblical Literature* (Grand Rapids, Mich.: Eerdmans, 1988, 1994); and *Preaching Christ from the Old Testament: A Contemporary Hermeneutical Method* (Grand Rapids, Mich.: Eerdmans, 1999).

Reformed exegesis. It is well known that Origen indulged in fantastic allegorizing to extract profitable spiritual lessons from what appeared to be unedifying Old Testament stories.[12] In this he was following the pattern of Stoic and Platonic philosophers who had allegorized Greek mythology. Philo used the same method in order to commend the Old Testament to cultured Hellenists. The Gnostics went to much greater excess as they used allegorizing to draw out secret doctrines that were not only absent from Scripture but contradicted it.

But, as Francis Foulkes points out, allegorizing as a method differs from typology, since it characteristically exegetes words rather than texts.[13] By assigning arbitrary meanings to words, the allegorist can avoid or subvert the meaning of the text.

Biblical hermeneutics, on the other hand, must take account of the text of Scripture, including the symbolism found in it. The Lord made us in his image, and the principle of analogy is fundamental in God's creation and revelation. Analogy always combines identity and difference. Interpretation may so press the identity as to reduce or remove the difference. This is the case in the Roman Catholic doctrine of transubstantiation: the Host is identified with the physical body of Christ. For the same reason, many were offended by Christ's teaching after his feeding of the five thousand. "How can this man give us his flesh to eat?" they asked (John 6:52, NIV). For these literal interpreters, Jesus was advocating cannibalism.

On the other hand, the aspect of identity cannot be ignored. That is the point of the comparison. Sometimes the text itself will assign meaning to a word, a fact that has been exploited by arbitrary allegorizing. When the Lord shows Jeremiah the rod of an almond tree to symbolize the sure fulfillment of his Word (1:11-12), the point is the word "almond." It means "watcher" (*shāqēd:* the almond is the "watcher" tree, heralding the approach of spring). God will watch

---

[12] See the fourth volume of his *De Principiis*, where he deals with the literal, moral, and allegorical interpretation of Scripture.

[13] Francis Foulkes, "The Acts of God: A Study of the Basis of Typology in the Old Testament," in G. K. Beale, ed., *The Right Doctrine from the Wrong Texts? Essays on the Use of the Old Testament in the New* (Grand Rapids, Mich.: Baker, 1994), 367.

over (*shōqēd*) his Word to fulfill it. So, too, the wonder of our addressing God as Father flows from the element of identity in the figure of Fatherhood.

Language itself is grounded in symbolism, and the human ability to employ symbols in contrast to animal response to signals remains the great distinction between human language and communication among animals.[14] In language we constantly use metaphors. We speak not only of a brave man being like a lion (a simile), but we call him a lion (a metaphor). Some metaphors have become "master metaphors" organizing a whole body of thought and practice. The term "body" has been used as a master sacramental metaphor in Roman Catholic ecclesiology. At the Second Vatican Council, the description of the church as the people of God as well as the body of Christ marked a departure from the exclusive use of the body metaphor. We may speak of discursive and presentational symbols.[15] Discursive symbols are linguistic. While they bring together incompatible spheres of thought, and carry suggestion beyond precise meaning, they do, nevertheless, communicate shared meaning which may be expressed in propositional form. Presentational symbolism, on the other hand, is the symbolism of art and of music: symbolism that is intuitive rather than discursive, having an emotional power rather than communicating rational meaning.

While the symbols of Scripture do evoke emotional response, they are also filled with discursive meaning. The vision of Ezekiel in the valley of dry bones is a compelling image. We even hear the rattling of the bones as they come together at the Word of the Lord. But the meaning of the vision is perfectly clear: the Lord has power to deliver his people from exile and fill them with new spiritual life. In the book of Revelation the images are discursive. They continue Old Testament images. The vision of Christ at the beginning of the book is not a representation of some archetypal dream image but a mosaic

---

[14] Ernst Cassirer, *Essay on Man* (New Haven, Conn.: Yale University Press, 1944), 26. This position has been supported in recent studies with primates.

[15] See Susanne K. Langer, *Philosophy in a New Key* (Cambridge, Mass.: Harvard University Press, 1957), chapter 4.

of Old Testament allusions that have meaning in revealing the glory of Christ.

While it must be granted that it is difficult to separate absolutely between meaning and significance, E. D. Hirsch, Jr., has well advocated the need for distinction.[16] Certainly, as interpreters of the Word of God, we must discover the meaning of the text and show its significance for our hearers. The Word of God has an established meaning, established by the primary Author as it is expressed through the inspiration of the Spirit. Further, the Spirit also interprets the Word to our understanding. In interpreting the symbolism of the Bible, we claim the doctrine of the perspicuity of Scripture. There are difficult passages; we may be uncertain or mistaken about the meaning of a passage, but Scripture is God's revelation, and workmen in the Word must seek his illuminating blessing.

Ceremonial Symbolism

Ceremonial symbolism in the Old Testament uses the fundamental distinction between the clean and the unclean. The comparison of sin to filth is linked with the need for cleanness to approach holy things or the holy Lord. The prevailing power of sin is shown in the fact that the unclean pollutes the clean, never the other way round. Haggai's message focuses on this feature (Hag. 2:10-14). In fulfillment, the prevailing power of Christ reverses the principle. When Jesus touches a leper, Jesus is not defiled, but the leper is cleansed and can claim his new status through the priest and sacrifice. This same reversal appears when Paul teaches that those converted to Christianity are not required to separate from their unbelieving spouses, as was necessary in the Old Testament. (Think of the reform among the returned Jews under Nehemiah, when those who had taken Gentile wives were required to divorce them.) The believer is to seek the conversion of the unbeliever, but in the meantime, the marital union is not to be thought of as making the Christian unclean. To the contrary, the

---

[16] E. D. Hirsch, Jr., *Validity in Interpretation* (New Haven, Conn.: Yale University Press, 1967); *The Aims of Interpretation* (Chicago: University of Chicago Press, 1976). See also Dan McCartney and Charles Clayton, *Let the Reader Understand* (Wheaton, Ill.: Victor, 1994).

unbeliever is cleansed insofar as that union is concerned, for the children who are the fruit of the union are holy (1 Cor. 7:14).

The whole sacrificial system, linked as it is with the dwelling of God in the temple among his people, is *sacramentally* symbolic, for it symbolizes the participation of the offerer in the benefit of the offering. The author of Hebrews describes at length the meaning of ceremonial symbolism and the building of the tabernacle "like in pattern to the true."

Prophetic symbolism must also be recognized in the Old Testament. We think of the relations between Hosea and Gomer; Jeremiah's buying a field in Anathoth (Jer. 32:9); Ezekiel's digging through the wall of his house to carry out his belongings as though fleeing into exile (Ezek. 12:5).

"Official" Symbolism

What we may call the symbolism of office appears everywhere in the Old Testament. A man may be presented as a sign (Zech. 3:8, *mophet,* almost = *typos).* The role of a king gives symbolic significance to his actions. David writes in the Psalms, not as a private individual but as the Lord's anointed servant. David becomes a figure for his coming Son, the Messiah (Isa. 55:3-5; cf. 11:1; Jer. 23:5-6; Ezek. 34:23). God warns Miriam and Aaron, "Why then were you not afraid to speak against my servant Moses?" (Num. 12:8, NIV). The office of the priest, involved as it is in ceremonial symbolism, is particularly marked out, and also points to the future (Zech. 3:8; 6:11-13). Even the nation has a role as God's son, his personal possession among the nations; Israel will either sanctify God's name or defame it by its behavior (Ezek. 36:16-38).

Historical Symbolism

The Old Testament also discerns the symbolic aspect of historical events, especially as these reveal God's ongoing work of redemption. God passes between the divided carcasses to take an oath to his covenant with Abraham; Abraham's actions contribute to the symbolism (Genesis 15).

Historical symbolism appears in Abraham's sacrifice of Isaac. On the one hand, it is clear that God's command to sacrifice Isaac was given to test Abraham. The passage begins with that statement of God's purpose (Gen. 22:1). Near the end of the passage, God says that he will bless Abraham because he has not withheld his only son (vv. 16-17). It has been argued, therefore, that to imagine any symbolism in the sacrifice of Isaac is importing into the text a meaning that is not to be found. Yet we must not skip over the name that is given to the event in the text. Abraham called the name of the place *Jehovah Jireh*—"the Lord will provide." An explanation is given: "As it is said to this day, In the Mount of the LORD it shall be provided" (v. 14, NKJV). The verb *jireh* is a form of a common verb for "see." The meaning "provide" or "see to it" is derived from the context in verse 8, where God's "seeing" the lamb is understood as providing it. More is involved here than simply the testing of Abraham's faith. The issue is the meaning of the sacrifice of Isaac. He, not Ishmael, is the seed of the promise. It is impossible that Isaac should be destroyed: "in Isaac your seed shall be called" (Gen. 21:12, NKJV). It is through the promised seed that redemption must come. The author of Hebrews takes seriously Abraham's word to the servants promising that *we* will return (Gen. 22:5). He interprets that to mean that Abraham was expecting to receive his son, if need be, by a resurrection from the dead (Heb. 11:17-18). The author adds that Abraham did, indeed, in a figure (*en parabolēi*) so receive him.

The place to which God directed Abraham is significant. The first use of the verb "to see" in Genesis 22 occurs in verse 4: "On the third day Abraham looked up and saw the place in the distance" (NIV). Abraham sees the ram caught in the thicket on the mount (v. 13). The place is again emphasized in the saying, "In the Mount of the LORD it will be seen," or "he will be seen."

Quite evidently there is significance in both the place and the seeing. Joining that to the significance of Isaac, we perceive that the Lord sees, or provides, a sacrifice as a substitute for Abraham's beloved son, at a place, and by a sacrifice, that are significant. Need we wonder that Paul alludes to this passage when he says, "He who did not spare his own Son, but gave him up for us all—how will he not also, along with him, graciously give us all things?" (Rom. 8:32, NIV).

God's final atonement for sin was not a ram caught in the thicket but the Son of the promise. Isaac could be spared, must be spared, for while he was the seed of the promise, he was so only in shadow, pointing to the true Seed, the beloved Son, not of Abraham but of the heavenly Father. God the Father spared the beloved son of Abraham but not his own Beloved.

MEMORIALS OF SIGNIFICANCE

The narrative of the testing of Abraham is one of a number in the Pentateuch where a place name or the name of an altar serves as a memorial, not merely to the event itself but to its meaning, its significance. So Jacob identified the dream God gave him at Bethel and the wrestling bout at the Jabbok, where his name was also changed (Gen. 28:19; 32:28, 30). The Passover proclaims the event of God's passing over the threatened houses of Israel because of the blood of the lamb. That event is woven together with the meaning of God's salvation (Ex. 12:11-14). The song of Moses on the other side of the Reed Sea again memorializes an event and becomes a promise of future deliverance. For that reason, God's coming great salvation is described as a second exodus (Isa. 40:3; 43:16; 52:12; Jer. 23:7-8; Hos. 2:14). In the wilderness, the Lord makes the experience of Marah to become an ordinance for Israel, full of future promise as well as present warning (Ex. 15:22-27). The gift of the manna, bread from heaven, was memorialized by divine command. A pot of manna was put before the tablets of witness in the ark of the covenant (Ex. 16:33-34). Later, Aaron's rod that budded was also placed there as a sign against the rebels who rejected God's choice of the high priest (Num. 17:10 [in Hebrew, Num. 17:25]).

In the same way, Moses names the altar that commemorates the victory over the Amalekites *Yahweh Nissi*, "The LORD is my banner"

(Ex. 17:15, ESV). He gives an explanation for the name: "A hand upon the throne of the LORD! The LORD will have war with Amalek from generation to generation" (v. 16, ESV). The term *nēs,* "banner" or "standard," alludes to the rod of Moses, which he held up, with support from Aaron and Hur, as he sat on a stone on a hilltop above the battle. As his hand held it aloft through the day, the army of Israel was given victory. "The Lord is my Banner" confesses that not the rod but the Lord himself is the sign of victory. The explanation shows this by affirming, "[There is] a hand on the throne of God," that is, it is not the rod of judgment in the hand of Moses that inflicted defeat on the Amalekites, but the uplifted hand of the Lord, holding, as it were, his rod of judgment.[17] (The Lord is on his throne; Moses, seated on the stone, must have appeared as enthroned above the battle.) The hand of the Lord is lifted to accomplish full and final judgment on Amalek.

The symbolism of the uplifted standard is continued in the prophets, where Isaiah applies it to the Root of Jesse, the Messiah (Isa. 11:10). Again a memorial name gives the symbolic significance of the event.

Another passage that shows the power of historical symbolism is the account of Moses' striking of the Rock at Massah/Meribah (Exodus 17). The key to understanding this passage is found in these names given to the incident. Both words are drawn from the account. Traveling at God's command in the wilderness, Israel encamped at Rephidim, where there was no water. Two terms are used to describe their complaint. The first verb is *rîb* (the root of "Meribah"), translated "quarreled" in verses 2 and 7 in the NIV. "Contend" would be better; the verb describes legal action. It means to sue, to bring charges in a lawsuit.[18] The noun is used later to describe the Lord's lawsuit against his people (Jer. 25:31; Mic. 6:1-8). The setting is the covenant relation between God and his people, already evident as

---

[17] The varying translations of the explanatory statement are due to different interpretations of what the uplifted hand of God means. It seems simplest to relate it to the imagery of the scene.

[18] H. B. Huffmon, "The Covenant Lawsuit in the Prophets," *Journal of Biblical Literature* 78 (1959): 285-295; B. Gemser, "The RiB or Controversy Pattern," in *Wisdom in Israel and the Ancient Near East,* Vetus Testamentum supplement III (Leiden, Netherlands: Brill, 1955).

they journeyed to Sinai. The people are charging God with breach of covenant: "Is the LORD among us or not?" (Ex. 17:7, NKJV).

Moses says, "Why do you contend with me? Why do you tempt the LORD?" (v. 2, NKJV). "Contend" is *rîb* again, while "tempt" is the verb *nasa* (in the participial form, "Massah"), which means "to test, to try, to tempt." In the context, this implies putting God on trial.[19]

Israel accuses God of abandoning them to die in the wilderness. They demand justice. Since God is not available to stand trial, they will accuse Moses in his stead. They are ready to stone him. Stoning, of course, is not mob violence but judicial execution by the community, with witnesses throwing the first stones. Moses understandably asks why they want to stone him. They have been brought to Rephidim by the word of the Lord. It is really against God that they are bringing charges.

Appreciation of this judicial setting enables us to understand what follows. The Lord tells Moses to take elders of the people with him, and his rod in his hand. The elders are the judges of Israel; they are to serve as witnesses for a court case. The rod of Moses is identified as the rod with which he struck the Nile River, turning it into blood. It is the rod of judgment: both a symbol of authority and an instrument for inflicting the penalty. We recall the fasces carried by the Roman lictors, a bundle of rods that were both symbols of authority and means of punishment.

Deuteronomy 25:1-3 describes the procedure for inflicting the penalty on the wrongdoer when a law-case is brought before the judges. The judges shall acquit the innocent and condemn the guilty. If the guilty man deserves to be beaten, the limit is set at forty blows.[20] Moses is to go before the people with the elders to convene a public trial. He will raise his rod of judgment to bring down a blow of justice upon the guilty. Isaiah describes the rod of the Lord descending

---

[19] In Psalm 78:15-20, Israel's testing of God with respect to water and food is expressed in terms of challenge: "Can God prepare a table in the wilderness? Behold, He struck the rock, so that the waters gushed out, and the streams overflowed. Can He give bread also?" (NKJV). Cf. Deuteronomy 6:16.

[20] The NIV translation assumes blows of a whip ("lashes"), but the Hebrew speaks only of striking blows.

in judgment upon Assyria: "Every stroke the LORD lays on them with his punishing rod will be to the music of tambourines and harps, as he fights them in battle with the blows of his arm" (Isa. 30:32, NIV).

Israel is guilty, but the rod of Moses is not raised against Israel. Instead, we have one of the most astonishing statements in the Bible. God says, "Behold, I will stand before you there on the rock at Horeb" (Ex. 17:6a, ESV).[21] In this trial scene, Moses stands with the rod of judgment in his hand, and God comes to stand before him! In judgment, men stand before God; God does not stand before a man. The law reads, "Then both men in the controversy shall stand before the LORD, before the priests and the judges who serve in those days. And the judges shall make careful inquiry . . ." (Deut. 19:17-18, NKJV).

Israel has called for justice, and the Lord brings the case to trial. He, the accused, stands in the prisoner's dock. His command to Moses is, "You shall strike the Rock." Moses dare not strike into the Shekinah glory of God's presence. But he is to strike the Rock upon which God stands, and with which he is identified. In the Song of Moses, God's name is "the Rock": "For I proclaim the name of the LORD: Ascribe greatness to our God. He is the Rock, His work is perfect" (Deut. 32:3-4a, NKJV). Jeshurun "forsook God who made him, and scornfully esteemed the Rock of his salvation" (v. 15, NKJV). "Of the Rock who begot you, you are unmindful, and have forgotten the God who fathered you" (v. 18, NKJV). "For their rock is not like our Rock, even our enemies themselves being judges" (v. 31, NKJV).[22] In two psalms that mention Massah and Meribah, God is called the Rock (Ps. 78:35; 95:1).

God is the Rock; he is not guilty, but he stands to receive the blow of judgment. "In all their affliction He was afflicted, and the Angel of His Presence saved them; in His love and in His pity He redeemed them, and He bore them and carried them all the days of old" (Isa. 63:9, NKJV).

God who is the Shepherd of his people not only leads them through the wilderness; he stands in their place that justice might be

---

[21] Literally, "Behold me, the one standing before your face there, upon the rock at Horeb."

[22] As this verse implies, the term "Rock" was used as a divine title in the ancient Near East.

done. The penalty is discharged: Moses strikes the Rock. The Lord redeems by bearing the judgment. From the smitten Rock there flows the water of life into the deadly wilderness. When Paul says the Rock was Christ (1 Cor. 10:4), he perceives the symbolism of the passage. Christ is present both in person and in symbol. In that incident, Christ the Lord stands on the Rock as the theophanic Angel, but the symbol of the Rock is needed to provide the symbol of that human nature he must assume to receive the atoning blow of judgment. We need not wonder at the severity of the Lord's censure of Moses when he struck the Rock a second time, unbidden (Num. 20:9-12).

ACTS AND WORDS OF THE LORD

The undergirding of historical symbolism is clear, and applies beyond those incidents where the symbolism is specifically named. God reveals himself in his saving deeds, and accompanies them with his promises. In that setting, God's deliverances of Israel anticipate his ultimate deliverance in the accomplishment of all his promises. The covenant form structures the future; the future fulfillment is in Christ, the Lord and the Servant.

Francis Foulkes spells out the witness of the Old Testament to its typological significance. He emphasizes the historical character of Old Testament revelation, and the consistency of God's nature and actions. God does, therefore, repeat his actions of blessing and of judgment. In the framework of the covenant, God's saving actions of the past are memorialized by the prophets, as well as by the marking of places by stones or altars, and of events by observances. God's covenant faithfulness becomes the ground of the promises of the inspired prophets about God's grace in the future. The acts of God are constantly accompanied by the word of God, declaring the meaning of what he has done and will do. Prophetic history is instructive, for it warns of the consequences of covenant breaking but extends again the wonder of God's plan and promise. The heightening of God's promise becomes the key to typology. God will not merely repeat his deeds of the past; he will do greater things, climactically greater: a second exodus, involving spiritual deliverance; a new covenant, a new creation, a new people, including Jews and Gentiles; and a greater than Moses, than David, than Elijah. The greater promise means that God himself must come, and the Servant of God must come, bearing the divine name.

Foulkes concludes that a type is "an event, a series of circumstances, or an aspect of the life of an individual or of the nation, which finds a parallel and a deeper realization in the incarnate life of our Lord, in his provision for the needs of men, or in his judgments and future reign."[23] "Deeper" is not strong enough here. It must be final and climactic, eschatological, Christocentric.

Warned by the arbitrary allegorizing of Origen, Reformed expositors have often shied away from typology. My own seminary teacher instructed us to recognize as types in the Old Testament only those things that are identified as types in the New Testament. That is certainly a safe rule. If the New Testament specifies something as a type, we may so interpret it. But that is a little like saying that you can find solutions to math problems only by looking in the back of the book, since you haven't a clue as to how to work the problems. To conclude that we can never see a type where the New Testament does not identify it is to confess hermeneutical bankruptcy. We know that New Testament writers did find types, but we confess that we cannot learn how they did it. There seem to be no discernible principles for us to follow.

There *is* a principle, however. Geerhardus Vos enunciated it when he said that the door to typology lies at the far end of the house of symbolism. That is, if there is symbolism in the account, we can rightly infer typology. If there is no symbolism, there can be no typology.

Symbolism, however, as we have seen, is not occasional in the Old Testament, but structural. God's acts point forward to his final salvation/judgment, and his relations with his people look forward to the restoration and renewal of the New Covenant.

---

[23] Foulkes, "Acts of God," 366.

With this in view, we can diagram the relation of symbolism to typology (see Figure 1, on this page).

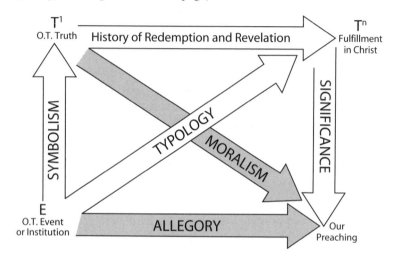

Figure 1

Where the symbolical appears, as in the incidents we have examined, the event or institution (E in the diagram) symbolizes a truth of God's revelation. We may call that truth, "truth to the first power" (T^1). That truth carries through to revelation in Christ, which we may call truth to the nth power (T^n). No revealed truth drops by the wayside in the course of God's redemption and revelation. All truths come to their realization in relation to Christ. If, therefore, we can construct a line of symbolism from the event or ceremony to a revealed truth, that truth will lead us to Christ. Here in Christ is that Truth in its fullness. Having constructed the two sides of a triangle in our theological geometry, we have also established the hypotenuse. That line is the line of typology.

We need also to drop a line down from T^n (the full revelation in Christ) to the present hearers of the message. This line starts with meaning in Christ, and is the line of significance. This is the line discerned by the interpreter.

Richard Craven at Westminster Seminary in Philadelphia once suggested to me two other lines that might be included in the diagram. I have shaded them in gray, for these represent illegitimate lines. The first brings down the line of significance on a diagonal, directly from the Old Testament revealed truth to us, with no reference to the fulfillment of the truth in Christ. This is the line of moralism. It presents a truth apart from the history of redemption and, therefore, apart from the cross, the resurrection, the ascension, the Lordship of Christ. It unconsciously assumes that we can go back to the Father apart from the Son.

Such an approach has been the bane of much preaching in the past, and of the time-honored way to tell Sunday school stories. David is presented as the brave little boy who was not afraid of the big bad giant, but who brought him down with his trusty slingshot. This approach has a little more difficulty with the story of David and Uriah, the husband of Bathsheba. But, of course, we may find moral examples that are negative rather than positive. Be brave, like David, but don't be an adulterous murderer like him. To be sure, the Bible shows strong disapproval of David's sin with Bathsheba and his order for the murder of Uriah.

The real problem comes, however, when Bible characters seem to be commended for doing dreadful things. Saul disobeys the Lord by not utterly destroying the Amalekites when the day of God's judgment against them comes (1 Samuel 15). Saul claims to have been perfectly obedient, and Samuel asks, "What about the bleating of sheep and lowing of cattle that I hear?" When Samuel learns that Saul has spared King Agag, he demands that the prisoner be brought in, and does to the king what Saul failed to do. He hews him to pieces before the Lord. Samuel's action, and its approval in the narrative, remains baffling on a moralistic level. To understand, we must take account of the history of redemption. Samuel's bringing down of the divine curse must be understood in the context of the Lord's conquering the enemies of his kingdom. The symbolism of the last judgment appears, as it does in all the wars of Israel, the true "holy wars" in which Israel fights, not for booty, but as God's avenging angel, bringing his judgment. The "jihad" or holy war that Islamic terrorists have waged against the United States is grounded in the Qur'an, which extends the Old Testament doctrine but denies the transformation of its fulfillment in Jesus Christ. Jesus, the risen and reigning Judge, withholds judgment for the accomplishment of his purposes of grace.

David goes against Goliath, not to display the courage of a young man but to fulfill the role of God's anointed. He had already been anointed by Samuel. For that reason, he cannot endure the blasphemies of Goliath. He describes Goliath's awesome armor, but says, "I come to you in the name of the LORD of hosts, the God of the armies of Israel" (1 Sam. 17:45, ESV). What David exhibits is faith. The author of Hebrews gives his roster of the men and women of faith in the Old Testament (Hebrews 11). Faith and grace go together. David as the Lord's anointed is a type of Jesus Christ, the Messiah, who meets and conquers Satan the strong man so that he may deliver those who are Satan's captives (Luke 11:15-19).

Moralism is inadequate as an explanation of Scripture; allegory is inadequate as well. The preacher relying on allegory will try to explain a text by picking something in it and giving it an interpretation that is unrelated to the context or meaning. For example, a preacher might take as a text the words "and a lamp" (2 Kings 4:10). The words describe part of the furnishings of a small room on the roof that a wealthy woman of Shunem built for Elisha so that he might be comfortable as he came by on his journeys. An allegorical interpretation might focus on the prophet's need for light, then make all sorts of applications, using the text as an excuse for a thematic message on spiritual light from Genesis to Revelation, using, no doubt, the lampstand in the tabernacle, and so forth. So, too, "a chair" might suggest the rocking chair of an aged parent, the high chair of a grandson, the father's chair at the head of the table, the empty chair of the prodigal son, and so forth.

Sidney Greidanus has greatly advanced the understanding and practice of Christ-centered preaching in his *Preaching Christ from the Old Testament*.[24] He outlines six ways or roads that the writers of the New Testament used to find types of Christ in the Old Testament.

---

[24] Sidney Greidanus, *Preaching Christ from the Old Testament;* and *The Modern Preacher and the Ancient Text.*

To these, Greidanus adds a seventh. Since the New Testament is complete, it provides a seventh way for us, namely, following its inter-pretation of the Old. The ways he lists are not ways that we may cre-ate to look back to the Old Testament to find Christ. Rather, they are roads along which the Old Testament leads us forward to Christ: They are: (1) the way of redemptive historical progression; (2) the way of promise-fulfillment; (3) the way of typology; (4) the way of analogy; (5) the way of longitudinal themes; (6) the way of contrast; (7) the way of New Testament references.

Greidanus's treatment of these ways is packed with rich insights. His distinctions overlap, however, and may be more simply grasped from the central teaching of the Old Testament about God's plan of salvation. That plan included God's promise at the beginning of the history of redemption, followed by epochs or periods in which his redeeming acts and words unfolded. The epochs must be empha-sized, for the longitudinal themes find expression in the contexts of the epochs. Dispensationalism fails to see the continuity of God's redeeming work, but biblical theology rightly sees the importance of the eras or epochs.

The Bible tells about God: God's redeeming acts, and God's words that interpret his deeds. The history of redemption is always accompanied by the history of revelation. We are told, for example, that in the sad period of the judges there was no frequent revelation (1 Sam. 3:1). The prophetic ministry given to Samuel showed that God had not forsaken his erring people. "For the LORD revealed Himself to Samuel in Shiloh by the word of the LORD. And the word of Samuel came to all Israel" (1 Sam. 3:21b–4:1a, NKJV).

The history of redemption is always accompanied by the history of revelation. God's interpretation of his own acts provides the themes that biblical and systematic theology gather and summarize. The longitudinal themes that Greidanus discerns are the themes found in the history of revelation. All God's revelation of himself necessarily involves analogy, as Cornelius Van Til constantly drove home. We are creatures, not the Creator, yet we are made in his image. As we saw earlier, symbolism rests on analogy. The contrast that Greidanus calls attention to is the great eschatological theme that joins the New Covenant to the Old. The heart of the contrast is marked by the coming of the Lord himself. Our situation is utterly hopeless. Only God can deal with it. His promise brings hope beyond all hoping, for he will come himself to redeem us. The Son of God appeared to Samuel, even as he had appeared to Moses in the burning bush. The Lord who spoke to Moses spoke also to Samuel and to the other prophets.

Isaiah speaks of the deliverance of Israel from Assyrian captivity as analogous to the exodus deliverance (Isa. 10:24-27). That prophecy, however, is swept up in the total realization and fulfillment of the coming of the Messiah, the Root (not just the Branch) of Jesse, who bears the Name, and is the Lord as well as the Servant. The gathering of Israel from exile will also bring the remnant of the nations to join the Israel of God.

The amazing promise of Isaiah 19 unfolds the triumph of God's saving purposes. In the day of the Lord, there will be an altar to the Lord in Egypt. The Assyrians will worship in Egypt, and the Egyptians will worship in Assyria, both passing by Jerusalem, for the worship in Jerusalem will be transcended in fulfillment. The precious names by which God addresses his own people will then be given to the enemy nations: "Blessed be Egypt my people, Assyria my handiwork, and Israel my inheritance" (Isa. 19:25, NIV).

The unfolding of the history of redemption and of revelation constantly binds together the words and deeds of the Lord. God is his own interpreter, and the climax of the day of the Lord foreseen in the prophets shows fulfillment that is not only restoration and renewal but transcending realization. The Lord himself will come, and will make all things new. Only the coming of the Lord can bring such realization, and nothing less will do. Augustine famously said of Adam's sin in the Garden of Eden, "Felix Culpa"—"fortunate transgression"! From the reality of the disaster of sin and death those words may be seen as blasphemous. Yet Augustine's point was the apostle Paul's: "What if God, choosing to show his wrath and make his power known, bore with great patience the objects of his wrath—

prepared for destruction? What if he did this to make the riches of his glory known to the objects of his mercy, whom he prepared in advance for glory—even us, whom he also called, not only from the Jews but also from the Gentiles?" (Rom. 9:22-24, NIV). Jesus saw the witness of the Old Testament to be a witness to his sufferings and the glory to follow. God alone could bring blessing to the objects of his infinite wrath; God alone could pay the price of redemption.

The Old Testament follows God's one great plan for human history and redemption, and the plan is not only from him, but centers on him: his presence in his incarnate Son.

The history of redemption and of revelation exists because of Christ's coming. Had Jesus Christ not been chosen in God's eternal plan, there would have been no human history at all. Adam and Eve would have fallen dead at the foot of the tree of the knowledge of good and evil. The grace of God's covenant promise is the source and heart of redemptive history. God declares, "I will walk among you and be your God, and you will be my people" (Lev. 26:12, NIV).

Possession marks the covenant relation. God redeems his people so that he may possess them. "For the LORD's portion is his people, Jacob his allotted inheritance" (Deut. 32:9, NIV). God claims Israel as his firstborn son and warns Pharaoh of his judgment on the firstborn sons of Egypt should he fail to let Israel go (Ex. 4:22-23). The Lord claims especially the firstborn sons of Israel. They represented all the other families of Israel. He spared them in the tenth plague on Egypt under the sign of the blood on the doorposts. The Levites, a tribe separated to serve the Lord at his tabernacle, were counted as substitutes for the firstborn sons. Beyond their number, every Israelite father paid five shekels to buy back his firstborn son (Ex. 13:15-16; Num. 3:14, 16, 42-51).

The Lord chose the people of his possession in love—not because they were more in number than other people but because he loved them. We hear the language of divine love: he loved them because he loved them! (Deut. 7:7-8). Further, God sealed his love to his people by his oath. The Old Testament term is *chesed,* an oath-bound commitment expressing freely given love. "Devotion" may be the best English translation. We would expect it to be used of the devotion of God's people for him. Judaism does use the term. The *Chasidim* are the devout ones. Yet the Old Testament uses the term almost exclusively for *God's* sovereign devotion to his own.

On the other hand, God's people possess him—but only because he gives himself to them: "I am the LORD your God . . ." From Mount Sinai God made his covenant with Israel. The Lord spoke the words of the Ten Commandments to the people below. For forty days, Moses remained on the mountaintop receiving from the Lord the design for the tabernacle. That was to be his tent in the midst of their tents. There God would dwell among them. He would possess them, and they him.

But when Moses came down from the mountain, he found Israel worshiping a golden bull as their god. Only Moses' own tribe, the tribe of Levi, was on the Lord's side. All the others were in full rebellion against Yahweh, the Lord they had vowed to serve. The Levites fought their brother tribes to end their revolt. God told Moses that he could not dwell in the midst of Israel. They were a stiff-necked people. He would lead them into Canaan and give them the land, but he could not dwell among them. It was too dangerous for them. His holy wrath would consume them in a moment. Moses prayed. He could not promise that Israel would do better. He could only plead that God would reveal his name to Moses, and show Moses his glory. God did so. He revealed his name as Yahweh the God full of *chesed* (covenanted devotion) and of truth—faithfulness. He promised to go in the midst of his people, and not just ahead of them. Moses prayed in thanksgiving. He repeated exactly what God had said. God had said, "Ye are a stiffnecked people; if I go up into the midst of thee for one moment, I shall consume thee" (Ex. 33:5, ASV). Moses prayed, "O Lord, let the Lord, I pray thee, go in the midst of us; for it is a stiffnecked people . . ." (34:9, ASV). The NIV changes this to *"although* this is a stiffnecked people" but this destroys the point of the exact repetition of the language. No, Moses repeats God's words, and adds, "and pardon our iniquity and our sin, and take us for thine inheritance."

Precisely because Israel is a stiff-necked people, they need the sovereign grace of the God who is "full of grace and truth." They need his dwelling in their midst, the tabernacle where God's glory rests. Yes, the Holy One must be screened off, but he has provided a way of approach: the altar of sacrifice, the cleansing laver, the light of the lampstand, the bread of the presence, the altar of incense— and the ark of the covenant for his throne. So John reflects on the fulfillment of the Lord's revelation to Moses: "The Word became flesh, and tabernacled among us (and we beheld his glory, glory as of the only begotten from the Father), full of grace and truth" (John 1:14, ASV margin).

Greidanus trenchantly asks, "Where did the New Testament writers, in contrast to their non-Christian Jewish counterparts, get the idea of interpreting the Old Testament from the reality of Christ?"[25] He gives an obvious answer first. The disciples had been with Jesus and had met the risen Lord. "But a more complete answer is that Jesus himself taught them to read the Old Testament in this way." Here is the key to our interpretation of the Old Testament. Jesus gave it to his disciples on Easter morning. He walked unrecognized with Cleopas and another disciple returning to Emmaus from Jerusalem. Seeing their sorrow and confusion, Jesus said, "'How foolish you are, and how slow of heart to believe all that the prophets have spoken! Did not the Christ have to suffer these things and then enter his glory?' And beginning with Moses and all the Prophets, he explained to them what was said in all the Scriptures concerning himself" (Luke 24:25-27, NIV).

Later, in the Upper Room, Jesus appeared to the disciples. He ate broiled fish in their presence to show the reality of the resurrection of his body, and said, "'This is what I told you while I was still with you: Everything must be fulfilled that is written about me in the Law of Moses, the Prophets and the Psalms.' Then he opened their minds so they could understand the Scriptures" (Luke 24:44-45, NIV). Luke then reports his words. Jesus provided a summary of the gospel and

---

[25] Greidanus, *Preaching Christ from the Old Testament*, 202.

its spread through the nations (vv. 46-47)—all from the Scriptures. This is to be the message of the disciples as his witnesses to all peoples. They are to wait for the empowering of the Spirit (vv. 48-49).

What Scriptures did Jesus speak of, then, during his ministry, to indicate their fulfillment?

From the beginning of his ministry to his ascension, Jesus constantly spoke of fulfilling the Scriptures—he ascends to heaven and is "lifted up" as Moses lifted up the serpent in the wilderness, and as Isaiah spoke of his being lifted up (John 3:14; 12:33-34; Prov. 30:4; Isa. 52:13). Jesus' announcement of the coming of the kingdom must be understood against the Old Testament climax of the promises in the coming of the Lord's reign of salvation. Jesus took from Daniel 7:13-14 his designation as the Son of Man who would come on the clouds of heaven (Matt. 24:30; Mark 14:62). In Daniel's prophecy the kingdoms of this world are likened to beasts emerging from the sea. Then there appears one like a son of man, coming with the clouds of heaven. He is given an eternal kingdom. Jesus linked his Son of Man title with his sufferings also. The contrast of his sufferings with the cloud of glory is part of the apparent paradox already evident in Isaiah 52:13-14.

Jesus also spoke of himself as the suffering Servant of Isaiah 53: "To be sure, Elijah does come first, and restores all things. Why then is it written that the Son of Man must suffer much and be rejected? But I tell you, Elijah has come, and they have done to him everything they wished, just as it is written about him" (Mark 9:12-13, NIV). On the cross, Jesus cried from Psalm 22:1, "My God, my God, why have you forsaken me?" (NIV). That cry was not *taken* from the psalm; it *fulfilled* the psalm. The graphic language of the psalm seems to go beyond any experience of David, and stands as prophecy of the crucifixion. While Jesus did not speak specifically of the dividing of his garments, the disciples knew he had fulfilled that psalm. The author of Hebrews quotes from the psalm to show that Jesus speaks of us as his brothers: "I will declare your name to my brothers; in the presence of the congregation I will sing your praises" (Ps. 22:22 as quoted in Heb. 2:12, NIV). Significantly, the passage attributes to Jesus the words of David throughout the psalm (not only the cry from the cross). The structure of Psalm 22 begins with the cry, then alternates between lament and confessions of trust, leading up to the cry for deliverance: "Come quickly. . . . Deliver my life. . . . Rescue me. . . ." Psalms that present the lament of an individual usually include a vow to give thanks when the answer comes (see Ps. 66:13-15). Also these psalms express assurance that the Lord has heard the cry and the vow: "You have heard me from the horns of the wild oxen" (Ps. 22:21, NIV margin). Usually the assurance of being heard is followed by verses of praise.

Jesus' fulfillment of Psalm 22 shows us much about the Christology of the Psalms. That psalm of the lament of the individual contains elements that may be found in other psalms. It includes expressions of trust, devotion in praise, as well as lament and cry for deliverance. Psalm 117 is a brief psalm of praise. Toward the end of the Psalter, praise fills the psalms. Psalm 23 is a distinct psalm of trust. There are also "we" psalms of lament (Psalm 79). Since Psalm 22 includes these varied elements, we have direction in understanding the references to Christ in similar psalms. The literary genre of the psalms does help us to see the continuity of forms that gives unity to the orientation of worship in Israel.

Beyond literary form we need also to consider the place of a psalm in the history of redemption. Here the superscription of the psalm often gives us direction, enabling us to fit the psalm into this history. A series of psalms of David from Psalm 51 to 63 follow his experiences (although not in historical order).

Jesus drew upon Psalm 110:1 to establish his deity. David called his son his Lord. Jesus asked his critics how they would explain that passage. How can David's son be his Lord? (Matt. 22:42-45; Mark 12:35-37; Luke 20:41-44).

When Jesus defended his disciples from the charge of Sabbath-breaking, he did not at all suggest that their plucking grain and rubbing off the chaff as they walked through a wheat field was too minimal to be regarded as reaping and winnowing. Instead he defended them by pointing to the privileges of David as the Lord's anointed, and the greater privileges that are his as the Lord of the Sabbath. So, too, the priests were without blame when they worked on the Sabbath. Those following Jesus on the Sabbath were follow- ing One who is greater than the temple. Jesus saw himself as fulfill- ing the symbolism of the temple as the dwelling of God with his people (Matt. 12:1-8; John 2:21).

Jesus said that Abraham had rejoiced to see his day (John 8:56). We think of Abraham's joy at the birth of Isaac. Nothing is impossi- ble for God (Gen. 18:14; Luke 1:37). Again Abraham rejoiced when Isaac was spared as the sacrificial lamb. Jesus did not identify himself, however, as merely a son of David or a son of Abraham. He is David's Lord, and he said, "Before Abraham was, I AM!" (John 8:58, NKJV).

Jesus' teaching about himself also included the wisdom literature of the Old Testament. When Jesus spoke of wisdom being proved right by her works, he used the feminine to speak of wisdom (Matt. 11:19). The Old Testament wisdom literature personified wisdom as a woman *(chokmâ* is feminine). Lady Wisdom is contrasted with Ms. Folly, the prostitute. Wisdom, God's personified attribute, was with God at the creation. Jesus praised his Father for hiding the mysteries of salvation from the wise and prudent and revealing them to babies. He then laid claim to infinite divine wisdom. "All things have been committed to me by my Father. No one knows the Son except the Father, and no one knows the Father except the Son and those to whom the Son chooses to reveal him" (Matt. 11:27, NIV).

When Jesus calls the weary and burdened to him, he issues the call of wisdom. He uses the language of the son of Sirach in Ecclesiasticus 51:23-27:

> Draw near to me, you who are untaught, and lodge in my school. Why do you say you are lacking in these things, and why are your souls very thirsty? I opened my mouth and said, Get [these things] for yourselves without money. Put your neck under the yoke and let your soul receive instruction; it is to be found close by. See with your eyes that I have labored little and found for myself much rest.

Compare the words of Jesus:

> Come to me, all you who are weary and burdened, and I will give you rest. Take my yoke upon you and learn from me, for I am gentle and humble in heart, and you will find rest for your souls. For my yoke is easy and my burden is light (Matt. 11:28-30, NIV).

Yet while the language is similar, the words of Jesus make a greater claim. Jesus is not another teacher of wisdom seeking disciples. He calls us, not to take the yoke of wisdom, as the son of Sirach did, but to take *his* yoke. He is calling the burdened to himself as the Son of the Father, who is the Wisdom of God. Hear again his claim: "All things have been committed to me by my Father. No one knows the Son except the Father, and no one knows the Father except the Son and those to whom the Son chooses to reveal him" (Matt. 11:27, NIV). In Christ all the treasures of wisdom and knowledge are hidden (Col. 2:2). Job's search for wisdom has ended, for the divine Wisdom calls (Job 28). Jesus is greater than Solomon. He fulfills the wisdom books of the Old Testament. The forms of teaching that Jesus used are the wisdom forms of the Old Testament, but he brings out of his treasures things new and old (Matt. 13:52). In him the Old Testament is made new in fulfillment, and the news of the gospel justifies the old, even as it fulfills and surpasses it.

At any point where we listen to the words of Jesus in the Gospels, we hear echoes of the Old Testament Scripture. On the Mount of Transfiguration, Jesus speaks with Moses and Elijah about his "exodus" that he must accomplish in Jerusalem. What they spoke of and anticipated, he fulfilled. As he rode into Jerusalem, the little children welcomed him and followed him into the temple, shouting, "Hosanna to the Son of David." When the priests and scholars told him to hush the children, Jesus quoted from Psalm 8, "From the lips of children and infants you have ordained praise" (Matt. 21:16, NIV). Again Jesus saw the fulfillment of Scripture, and indeed, from his own infant praises to his blessing as he ascended, *all* Jesus' words were fulfilling the Scriptures.

While Greidanus might have drawn together his separate "ways" to advantage, he opens the doors to textual interpretation that focuses on the meaning of the text to Israel, the original hearers. Even this commitment to original meaning cannot be made supreme in application to the Word of God. The prophetic richness of Old Testament Christology goes beyond any grounding in the address to Israel. There was much that even David the king did not understand in his own writings. The witness of the Scriptures to Christ is the reason they were written—and of him and through him and to him are all things (Rom. 11:36). Greidanus rightly insists on careful literary explanation, but concerning Jesus Christ, as I am sure Greidanus realizes more than I, there is a fullness that can never be comprehended.

2

PREPARING A SERMON THAT PRESENTS CHRIST

GOSPEL PREACHING PRESENTS Jesus Christ. The apostle Paul asks the foolish Galatians, "Who has bewitched you? Before your very eyes Jesus Christ was clearly portrayed as crucified" (Gal. 3:1, NIV). Paul attacks the "false apostles" who perverted the good news of salvation in Christ into a plan for earning heaven. He does not only declare that God saves by grace, not works; he brings Christ forward, and placards him. Preaching points to Christ crucified for our sins, and risen for our life.

Preaching in the power of the Holy Spirit is preaching in the presence of Jesus. When Paul speaks of Christ's triumph over the powers of darkness, he is aware of the presence of the demonic astral forces. Our country was shocked when Muslim terrorists used airliners to destroy the twin towers of the World Trade Center in New York and to slash destruction into the Pentagon. Yet we still live without awareness of the struggle for which the Lord armed Paul. Jesus conquered on the cross those powers of Satan and his angels. Paul sees Christ crucified. The Romans often nailed to the cross of a condemned criminal his handwritten confession. Paul sees the cross of Jesus, and nailed to it the handwritten sins and crimes of those for whom he died (Col. 2:14-15). Paul describes the meaning of the atonement, but never in abstraction from the real presence of Jesus— on the cross, and in the preached word. "Show us Jesus" is a fit motto for Sunday school teachers and for preachers.

THE LORD HIMSELF SPEAKS IN PREACHING

His Call Is Heard

Paul has told us the secret of preaching. He begins by affirming, "Whosoever shall call upon the name of the Lord shall be saved." He asks, "How then shall they call on him in whom they have not believed? and how shall they believe in him whom they have not heard? and how shall they hear without a preacher?" (Rom. 10:13-14, ASV). This passage has often been translated, "how can they believe in the one *of whom* they have not heard." *"Whom* they have not heard" is the right translation. (Verbs of hearing in Greek use the genitive as the direct object.) In the preaching of the gospel, Christ himself speaks to those who hear.

The New Testament uses many terms for preaching. Preaching includes proclaiming the Good News, teaching the richness of God's revelation, encouraging, exhorting, warning, and rebuking. Yet no aspect of preaching may lose sight of the call of the Savior. Some preachers draw the weak and weary to Christ, others drive rebels to seek refuge from the wrath of the Lamb on the throne. Both tender entreaty and stern warning come from the lips of the personal Savior who speaks through his preached Word.

Bible Study Draws Us to His Presence

Do you need reminding to be aware of the presence of the Lord as you study his Word? Of course, reading his Word is also the prime way of seeking his presence. How do we ever manage to forget that it is the Lord who addresses us?

Vern Poythress has analyzed the structure of discourse.[1] He shows that meaning is a static element. There is a fixed meaning. This, of course, is denied in postmodern thinking. It is now supposed that the only meaning that exists is the meaning taken (or given) by someone. Bible study groups practiced this long

---

[1] Vern S. Poythress, "A Framework for Discourse Analysis: The Components of a Discourse from a Tagmemic Viewpoint," *Semiotica* 38, no. 3/4 (1982): 277-298; "Hierarchy in Discourse Analysis: A Revision of Tagmemics," *Semiotica* 38, no. 1/2 (1982): 107-137.

before we thought of ourselves as postmodern. The meaning of a text was bounced around in Bible study groups: "To me, this text means that . . ." No one can deny such claims. Yet the question remains, Is the claim mistaken? Does the text mean that, or has it been misunderstood? It is fascinating to read the injured replies of some who deny fixed meaning when *they* claim to have been misunderstood!

Meaning is also drawn into the dynamic of communication: the sender, the message, and the receiver. Further, the relational element provides the context of communication. The setting of the message includes those to whom it is addressed, but has significance beyond those for whom it was originally intended.

Since we are concerned about presenting Jesus, we might want to break down the walls of textual meaning to get to the goal of our relation with the Lord. Dreary exegesis and word studies seem to rise like a rocky mountain, a barrier rather than a road in our impatience to reach the top of the Mount of Transfiguration.

Yet the opposite is the case. I recall hearing Tim Keller of Redeemer Presbyterian Church in Manhattan describing the path of devotion. He insisted that Scripture opens the door of heaven to those who seek the Lord. Mystics through the centuries have described the disciplines by which they have attempted to climb "Jacob's ladder." They agree that these practices may bring us to the gate of heaven, but that the gate must be opened from the other side. Ascetic abstinence cannot produce spiritual reality. The monks of Mount Athos at the end of the second millennium repeated the Jesus prayer as a mantra. No doubt they were able to pray sincerely, "Jesus, Son of God, have mercy on us," many times over. Yet constant repetition causes rational thought to spin out and isolates intuitive consciousness. This consciousness differs from the deepening of understanding and faith that brings mind and heart to the presence of the Lord. Hearing the Word of the Lord is an exercise in faith—in believing that the Lord does hear and answer our plea. The Lord's communion with us is personal. Its intensity goes beyond our expressions of devotion, but our words and our cries answer to his address of love.[2]

To see how study of the text of Scripture draws us to the presence of the Lord, consider a passage that expresses his love. The Lord says to us, "I have loved you with an everlasting love; therefore with lovingkindness I have drawn you" (Jer. 31:3, NKJV). The word of the Lord is addressed to the virgin of Israel. It expresses his covenant love. That love is sworn devotion. The term "lovingkindness" in the NKJV translates *chesed.* The God of *chesed* is the God who has sealed with his oath his pledge to be the Savior of his own. In Genesis 15 we read of the self-maledictory oath that God took in becoming the God of Abraham. To keep his oath, God himself came to be the Savior of his people.

Attention to Scripture shows us that God's expression of his love binds his love to his chosen people. God came down in his love to show his devotion to his own. He appeared to Abraham and to his offspring as the Angel of the Lord. The Lord's devotion, his *chesed,* is profoundly personal, but is directed to his chosen people. We who are chosen in Christ share the love that is given us for Christ's sake, as members of his body. No believer can boast of an isolated communion with Christ. The popular hymn declares, "I come to the garden alone, while the dew is still on the roses. . . . The joy we share as we tarry there, none other has ever known." This boast runs against the grain of biblical piety. The Lord does speak of his tender silence in his love for his people, and his rejoicing over them with singing (Zeph. 3:17). Yet it is *his people* rather than isolated individuals that the Lord addresses. Sentimental romanticism strays far from the response of faith to the reality of God's love.

Careful, devout reflection on the Word of the Lord remains the key to entering his presence in worship.

---

[2] See E. P. Clowney, *CM★: ★Christian Meditation* (Nutley, N.J.: Craig, 1978).

STRUCTURE THE SERMON TO PRESENT CHRIST

The Explanation/Application Division Is Transformed by the Presence of Christ

IN THE VARIETY OF THE WORDS AND WORKS OF JESUS

Sermons have often been divided between explanation and application. Another strategy saves application for the conclusion. To avoid this bunching, brief applications may be appended to the separate points. Too often, this results in a series of sermonettes loosely connected to the theme.

Presenting Christ in the message dissolves this problem, for now we present Jesus both in what he says and does to reveal *himself,* and in what he says and does to direct *us.* Once again, the presence of Jesus unifies our message as we hear him. For our hearers to be aware of Jesus, we must not neglect to preach from the Gospel narratives. A vivid sense of the presence of Jesus rests on our becoming acquainted with how he acted in his earthly ministry and what he said to the crowds, to his disciples, to his critics, and to his Father in heaven. It is the real Jesus whose presence we know by faith. Preaching the Lord as present in the Gospel narratives has more power than do the best films that seek to portray the ministry of the Lord. The *Jesus* film distributed internationally by Campus Crusade has presented the gospel to vast crowds, including thousands in pre-literate societies. Yet it is deeply flawed in its conclusion at this very point: the presence of Jesus. An actor pleads with the viewer to come to *him* and to trust in *him.* The effort to give reality beyond the preached word fails as fiction. The actor is not Jesus.

This warns us preachers. We cannot enact the role of Jesus, nor his facial expression as he spoke. The reality of Jesus cannot use a stand-in.

IN THE TRANSCENDENCE OF CHRIST'S HEAVENLY GLORY

No less do we need the descriptions of the glory of Jesus in the Epistles. In those inspired letters, the reality of his bodily resurrection and heavenly glory draws us to Jesus who is the same yesterday, today, and forever (Heb. 13:8).

Our presentation of Jesus takes account of the confession of the church through the ages. Salvation has always meant our being united to Christ by faith. We know him as our Mediator, our Prophet, Priest, and King in his ministry on earth and in his glory above. On the cross he represented us, and from the throne he comes to us as his Spirit. Read Paul's letter to the Philippians and see how his immediate awareness of Jesus breathes through the whole letter. The Gospel of John shows us how the words of Jesus accompany the great deeds that were the signs of his coming.

We rightly prize doctrinal preaching. We need to instruct the church concerning the person and work of Jesus. Now as ever, false gospels abound. Yet we lose the reality of the Lord if we lose our focus on the reality of his presence. Cataloging errors will not serve if we warn of Pelagius or Arminius but do not show the glory of the Lord whose word they failed to understand.

Sermon Structure Presents Christ in the Story of Redemption

All presentation of Jesus has a narrative dimension. His coming brings the climax to the great story of the Bible. In the Old Testament Jesus appears as the Angel of the Lord, identifying himself as the "I AM" God (Ex. 3:2, 14). Isaiah saw his glory in the temple. As we have seen, John identifies the glorious Lord whom Isaiah saw in a vision as Jesus (John 12:41, NIV).

The Old Testament narratives describe the coming of the Lord as his being present with the seed of the promise. When Abram entered the land of Canaan at God's direction, the Lord appeared to him at the oak in Shechem and promised to give him the land. Abram built an altar to memorialize God's appearing. Later, God appeared in flame to pass through the divided carcasses—a symbolic appearing that, as we have seen, marked God's oath sealing his covenant with Abram. Still later, the Lord came with two angels and promised what was impossible to men, that aged Sarah would have a son. God brought joy to Abraham and Sarah when Isaac was born. The Lord then asked of Abraham that he sacrifice Isaac, the son he loved. But Isaac could not be the sacrifice for Abraham's salvation. When Abraham stretched out his knife to slash his son's throat, the Lord stayed his hand. The Lord provided a substitute, a ram caught in the bushes.

In the life of Jacob the Lord again came down to be present, and to renew his covenant promise. When Jacob had received his father's blessing, his brother Esau threatened to kill him, and Jacob fled. At Bethel (Gen. 28:10-22), the Lord came down to repeat his promise. As we have seen, this appearing of the Lord to Jacob says that the Lord stood over him. In Jacob's dream God came down the stairway to stand over Jacob. (See Genesis 35:13, where, again at Bethel, "God went up from him.") He came down the stairway in his own presence to be with Jacob, and promised never to leave him. It was the Second Person of the Trinity, the Son of God, who stood over Jacob. Always the presence of the Lord appears in the coming of the Son, the Revealer of the Father. Jesus speaks of this passage when he tells Nathanael that he will see heaven opened and the angels of God ascending and descending on the Son of Man (John 1:51). It would seem that Jesus is not likening himself to the stairway, but referring to himself as the one on whom the angels had ascended and descended when he came down at Bethel. They will again attend him at his second coming, when he comes in glory.

The presence of the Lord was shown dramatically when the Lord came down to wrestle with Jacob at the Jabbok River. Jacob was returning at God's direction after his years with Laban in Haran. He dreaded his meeting with Esau, from whose anger he had fled. Two companies of angels met Jacob as he entered the land; then the Lord met him in a wrestling match. The wrestling of champions had a place in ancient Near Eastern religious literature. We must not think of the buffoonery of wrestling on television. In Jacob's match, both won by losing. Jacob lost when the Lord touched his hip, but Jacob won because he would not let go. The

Lord lost in a sense when he blessed Jacob; but he won, because blessing Jacob was his final purpose. Jacob was lamed in his "hip." When Jacob's "hip" is spoken of in two other passages, it refers to Jacob's seed, his offspring. The symbolism of the seed of Jacob points to Christ, who was "pinned" on the cross for us. In the early dawn Jacob could discern the face of the Angel. He called the place Peniel, for he said, "I have seen God face to face, and my life is preserved" (Gen. 32:30, ASV).

All through the Exodus narrative the presence of the Lord is revealed to Israel. At the burning bush the Angel of the Lord spoke to Moses. When Moses asked for his name, the name the Angel gave was Yahweh, the "I AM" God. The Lord said he had heard the groaning of his people in their bondage, and had come down to save them. The Lord does not save from a distance but in his own presence. In the pillar of fiery cloud, the presence of the Lord led his people out of Egypt. When the Egyptians pursued, the Lord's cloud became a curtain of flame to shield Israel from their chariots. The Lord looked out of the cloud to bring destruction on the Egyptian chariotry as they attempted to follow in the path the Lord had opened in the sea.

When the Lord brought Israel to Sinai, he said, "I carried you on eagles' wings and brought you to myself" (Ex. 19:4, NIV). The fear of Israel was fear of God's presence when they stood before him where his cloud covered the mountain.

In the passages describing the Exodus, God came down in the cloud of his presence to lead and protect his people. We remember that the cloud of fire screened off Israel from the pursuit of Egyptian chariotry. On Mount Sinai, Moses received the plans for the tabernacle, the tent of God pitched in the midst of the camp of Israel. Yet even as Moses was receiving those plans, the people were worshiping before a golden bull they had made.

After that idolatry, God said that he could not dwell in the midst of the people. The design Moses received from God put the tabernacle in the center of the tribal encampment. The tribes, by their clans, were to raise their standards all around God's tent, with the priests and Levites encamped to the east, in front of the tabernacle. They were a "stiff-necked" people (like a horse that resisted its bridle). For him to dwell in a tent in the middle of their camp was too dangerous for them. The flame of his holiness could burst forth and consume them.

God said that he would not live in the middle of their tents, but that he would go before them. He would drive out the Canaanites from the Promised Land, but he would not dwell "among" them (Ex. 33:3, ESV). "In the midst" translates the Hebrew term more pointedly. If God's presence was not to be in their midst, God would need no tent among them. The tabernacle would not be needed.

When the Lord said that his presence would not go with them, Moses replied that there was then no point in their going on. He led Israel in mourning, and prayed. He prayed that the Lord would proclaim his name again to Moses, and show Moses his glory. Both the name of the Lord and the glory of the Lord were expressions of his presence. God heard the prayer of Moses and proclaimed his name as Yahweh, full of *chesed* and *'emet*, covenant love and faithfulness (grace and truth). God showed his glory to Moses, passing by Moses hidden in the cleft of the rock.

In John's Gospel, John uses the Greek word that could be translated "tabernacled" or "tented." John refers to Exodus 34:6 in John 1:14. In the prayer of Moses, he repeats God's words that he cannot go in the midst of this stiff-necked people, but adds, "and pardon our iniquity and our sin, and take us for your inheritance" (Ex. 33:5; 34:9, ESV).

The whole passage is the turning point in the book of Exodus. After the Lord promises that his presence will be with them, the people give generously for the tabernacle; it is built exactly according to the divine plans, and the book concludes with the glory of the Lord's presence filling the Holy of Holies. The whole book of Exodus is about the Lord's presence, delivering, guiding, then dwelling with his people. As the reference in John 1:14 indicates, all this points forward to the incarnate coming of the presence of the Lord.

Christ also revealed himself in the types of Old Testament symbolism. Through the Old Testament story we hear not only about the presence of the Lord but also about the coming of the Servant of the Lord, foreshadowed in those who served in his covenant. The elaborate symbolism of the ceremonial law no longer offers a handbook for ritual, since Christ has come. Rather, we are drawn from the shadows into his light, the light of his presence.

The symbolism of the Apocalypse presents Christ by harvesting Old Testament images in John's visions on the Isle of Patmos. Preaching from the book of Revelation has gained much from recent study. The commentary of Dennis Johnson has shown the symbolism of Revelation in the setting of the history of redemption.[3] Proclamation of the present saving rule of Christ needs clear emphasis because of the advances of Islam and the wars in the Middle East.

Direct Discourse Presents Jesus

Jesus is present when he reveals himself to us and also when he speaks to instruct, guide, and warn us. When preaching from Gospel accounts, do not put the words of Jesus into indirect discourse. Call on your hearers to hear the words of Jesus, and quote them. "How shall they believe in him whom they have not heard?" Jesus speaks in preaching. Red-letter Testaments have been condemned for suggesting that the quoted words of Jesus are somehow more authoritative than the Gospel record that reports them. Both are Scripture, the Word of God. Yet the apostle Paul quoted the words of the Lord Jesus when he instituted the Lord's Supper (1 Cor. 11:23-25). Max Maclean's reading of the Gospel of Matthew rings with Jesus' accusations as the Lord rebuked the unbelief of his opponents. The presence of Jesus proved to be most uncomfortable for the Pharisee who had invited Jesus as a dinner guest (Luke 7:36-47). We dare not soften in preaching the warnings that Jesus speaks when he is present in the Spirit.

---

[3] Dennis Johnson, *The Triumph of the Lamb* (Nutley, N.J.: Presbyterian & Reformed, 2001).

PRAYER PREPARATION TO PRESENT CHRIST

Seeking the Unction of the Presence of Jesus

Pray not in general for the Lord's blessing on your message, or for unction as enablement of your speaking. As you commune with the Lord in prayer, seek his presence. Ask for awareness of him as you look at the people to whom you speak. It is true that the Lord will disclose his presence through his Word. The power is his, and your state of sanctification, as you well know, does not limit the effectiveness of your message. You and I can both recall preaching that never got airborne but was used to open the eyes of faith.

On one occasion I had tea with Martyn Lloyd-Jones in Ealing, London, and decided to ask him a question that concerned me. "Dr. Lloyd-Jones," I said, "How can I tell whether I am preaching in the energy of the flesh or in the power of the Spirit?"

"That is very easy," Lloyd-Jones replied, as I shriveled. "If you are preaching in the energy of the flesh, you will feel exalted and lifted up. If you are preaching in the power of the Spirit, you will feel awe and humility."

The Lord, in his mercy, showed me what Lloyd-Jones meant. I was in London on my way to Schloss-Mittersill, a castle in Austria owned by InterVarsity Christian Fellowship. I was to speak there at a student conference. Some of the students at the conference were American, but others were from countries then behind the Iron Curtain. One afternoon I met with the group to speak. The venue was a tower room in the castle. A great fire was blazing in the hearth. The students had been hiking in the mountains, and trickled in to hear a message before dinner. The room was hot. They were sleepy, and so was I. But I did present Jesus to them. I was not in the least prepared for what happened. As I finished, many students began to weep. Some fell on their knees to pray. They continued to pray, and I sat down to pray with them. After a time the dinner bell rang from the dining room below.

Being unaccustomed to revivals, I did not want to prolong the time artificially. I decided I had better go down so as not to interfere with the food service. I did go down, but when I did, no one else came. I don't know how long it was that I sat in the empty dining room before anyone else came down. Perhaps it was only fifteen or twenty minutes.

Now I knew what Lloyd-Jones meant. I was filled with awe.

Practicing the Presence of the Lord

The point of this section is well made in the notable booklet with that title.[4] Jesus rebuked his disciples for their little faith when they doubted his reality as he came walking on the water to them. "It is a ghost," they cried out in fear (Matt. 14:26, 31, ESV). Before he went to the cross, Jesus told his disciples that he must leave them and go to the Father. But he added that he would not leave them as orphans, but come to them (John 14:18). After the resurrection, Jesus told them to wait for the promise of the Father. That promise was the coming of the Spirit in whom Jesus would come to them. That is why the book of Acts continues the story of what Jesus began to do and teach after he was lifted up (Acts 1:4). He did that in the Spirit, who rested on believers. It is why the Epistles tell of our union with Christ. Paul speaks often of believers being "in Christ." Union with Christ joins us to one another in his body (Eph. 2:13-16), the church.

In the Psalms, David and other psalmists seek the presence of the Lord in his tabernacle, but also sing under the shadow of his wings in wilderness experiences. What the psalmists sought is what we are given as Christians when our bodies are made the temple of the Holy Spirit. The Epistles are full of the indicatives of our salvation. The Lord is with us, and we are with him. Nothing can separate us from him, or from his presence. We are called therefore to live with the Lord who lives in us by his Spirit. The peace of God that passes all understanding is the peace of his presence.

Practicing God's presence therefore means acknowledging what we know to be so. We live in a world that is groaning, awaiting the

---

[4] Brother Lawrence of the Resurrection, *The Practice of the Presence of God,* trans. John J. Delaney (New York: Doubleday, 1996).

redemption of the sons of God. We ourselves groan in the midst of sorrows and suffering. But the Holy Spirit groans in us and with us. Nothing can separate us from our Savior's love. We cast our cares on him, for he cares for us.

Preaching in the Presence of the Lord

As we seek to present Jesus in our preaching, we do not have the gifts and calling of the apostle Paul. But we do portray Christ crucified before the very eyes of our hearers. Trust him. The same Lord is present with us. The disciples asked the risen Lord if he would at that time restore the kingdom to Israel. Jesus left with the Father the times and seasons of his plan. To their question about the kingdom, Jesus answered with the Father's promise of the Spirit (Acts 1:8; John 14:16). Jesus had been teaching them through the Spirit, and the Spirit would continue to teach them. Jesus is the Truth, and his Spirit witnesses to the truth.

The book of Acts shows how the Spirit of Truth guided the apostolic church in the light of the Lord's revelation. They knew the presence of the Lord among them, for they understood that in the Spirit Jesus came in person to continue the things he had done and taught before he ascended. Their witness in Judea, Samaria, and to the ends of the earth continues in the power of the Spirit till Jesus comes again.

Distinctive apostolic gifts were given for the foundation of the church. Paul's distinctive gifts marked his apostleship (2 Cor. 12:12). His calling as the Apostle to the Gentiles gave him the message that he could call "my gospel" (Rom. 2:16; 16:25; 2 Thess. 2:8). He labored to lay the foundation on which others would build. He was "a minister of Christ Jesus to the Gentiles with the priestly duty of proclaiming the gospel of God, so that the Gentiles might become an offering acceptable to God, sanctified by the Holy Spirit" (Rom. 15:16, NIV). His power in the Spirit was power in the presence of the Lord. He saw all his service as worship. For him to live was Christ. For Jesus his Lord he had suffered the loss of all things that he might know him (Phil. 3:8-9).

Preaching in the presence of the Lord is more personal than possessing power in expression, a power that might be thought of as unction for the task. James McConkey, writing about victorious living, likened the power of the Spirit to the water pressure in a great dam.[5] Our act of consecration turns open the valve to allow the power of the Spirit to flood into our lives. Another of McConkey's illustrations was more dated. He likened the Spirit's power to the current in the electric cable above a trolley car. Put the wheel of the car's rod on the cable, and the current would surge into the motor. These illustrations misconceive the personal presence of the Spirit of Jesus. I had to learn again that my salvation comes, not by my grip on him, but by his grip on me. The Lord saves us by the wonder of his own personal presence with us. So it is with preaching. We do not seek a surge of power in ministering the Word of God. We seek his presence in the act of preaching, as we hold forth the person of Jesus Christ.

Self-consciousness always threatens our presenting Christ. We cannot hold him forth if we lack awareness of his presence. Looking to the Lord himself is the answer. Turn the eyes of your hearers to look at him. Use dialogue. What are your hearers saying to the Lord? Quote what they may be thinking. Think of how the Lord's Word is addressed to a person in the congregation or audience. Imagine what some of your hearers may be saying to the Lord, and declare his answer from his Word. You are mediating a conversation of a saint and sinner with the Lord himself. Remember that his Word does not return empty, and that he is speaking it. Keep your language vivid, not by illustrations and figures of speech that steal attention from him, but by vivid references to what the Lord says and does. Be sure that illustrations do not distract from what they illustrate. Catch attention with a story about a sports or music idol, and you may never get it back.

Such advice is not new. What is new and fresh in your preaching is the devotion with which you look to the Lord to present himself to you and to your hearers.

---

[5] James McConkey, *The Three-fold Secret of the Holy Spirit* (1897; reprint Lincoln, Nebr.: Back to the Bible, 1977).

3

SHARING THE FATHER'S WELCOME

(Luke 15:11-32)

AMERICANS HAVE TAKEN to hanging up yellow ribbons along with the red, white, and blue. It all began at the outset of Ronald Reagan's presidency, when the hostages were released from Iran. They were welcomed with yellow ribbons fluttering from trees and utility poles in Washington, D.C., and on Main Street U.S.A. The image came from a popular ballad about a wife signaling a welcome to her husband, just released from jail, by tying a yellow ribbon "'round the old oak tree." The song has mercifully faded, but the symbol has caught on. The yellow ribbon has become our sign of a joyful welcome home.

One of the stories that Jesus told gives us the picture of a yellow ribbon tied across the open gate of heaven. Jesus described the joy of heaven in welcoming home a penitent sinner. The familiar story is often called the parable of the prodigal son. Some have said it might better be called the parable of the elder brother, since it ends with his reaction to his brother's homecoming. But the central figure in the story is the father, who would welcome both sons to his feast. Jesus tells the story so that we might understand the welcome of his heavenly Father and join in its joy.

In the first part of his story, Jesus shows the *grace* of the Father's welcome; in the second part he tells us about the *demand* of that welcome.

THE GRACE OF THE FATHER'S WELCOME

The story begins with the younger of two brothers. This youth is living at home and hating every minute of it. Everything turns him off: the household, the farming, the lifestyle of his father. There is only one thing about his father that he does like: the old man's money. But the prospects of cashing in on it are remote. His father shows no sign of an early decease. At last the young man's patience runs out. "Father," he says, "give me what's coming to me from your estate."

It would be a rude demand in any society; it was especially harsh in view of the Old Testament laws of inheritance. Jewish wisdom, too, advised fathers against dividing their holdings before the day of their death: "For it is better that your children ask of you than that you should look to the hand of your sons" (Ecclesiasticus 33:22). But the father does what his younger son asks. He divides his estate. The young man finds himself holding title to at least a third, perhaps half, of his father's living. He gathers it all together. That is, he converts it into cash, so that he can put it in a bag and pull the string around it. Now he has what he has always wanted. He can go where he wants and do what he wants.

He does.

He leaves home at once; every step is a step into freedom, so he keeps on traveling. With a world of distance between him and his father's house he can live a little.

In the Sunday school of my childhood there were varnished oak chairs set in circles and pictures on the painted walls. They were all Sunday school pictures. In the basement, though, behind a door to a corridor, there was an engraving that didn't look like a Sunday school picture at all. It showed the prodigal son at a party. Some party. It didn't occur to me when I peered at the picture, but no doubt the prodigal picked up the tab.

In his story, Jesus does not give any details as to how the prodigal spent his money. Did months or years pass before his high living had to be scaled down? Did his funds evaporate in a rush, or did he ration sin on a budget? In any case, at last it was no more a question of the cheapest wineshops or the cheapest women. It was the question of a crust of bread. The prodigal was penniless just as a famine struck the country, inflating the price of food. His wasted inheritance had bought him no friends. He had to get a job if he were not to starve, and the only job he could get was as a swineherd, feeding pigs. The point is not that feeding pigs is a messy occupation. The point is that pigs are an unclean animal in the technical sense of Old Testament law. Every bond with his father's house was broken. The prodigal was an alien, far from home, estranged, lost, unclean.

The prodigal's repentance is not glamorized in the parable. It began not in the depths of his heart but in the pit of his stomach. He watched the pigs crunch the dry carob pods that he fed them. His meager earnings could not provide him with daily bread, especially at famine prices. Perhaps he could manage carob pods. They were, after all, edible. How hungry he was! What meals he used to enjoy! His mind went back, not to the luxurious banquets that had cost him his inheritance, but to the dinners in his father's house. His father's house! "How many of my father's hired men have food to spare, and here I am starving to death!" (Luke 15:17, NIV).

Yes, he had said it aloud. It was true. He had been a fool, and a wicked fool at that. "He who keeps the law is a discerning son, but a companion of gluttons disgraces his father" (Prov. 28:7, NIV). He had to go home. He had to face his father again. What could he say? "Father, I have sinned against heaven and against you. I am no longer worthy to be called your son; make me like one of your hired men" (Luke 15:18-19, NIV).

His father would take him in and give him employment and food. He was sure of it. He had no right to claim the old relationship, but he could see again his father's face.

The prodigal's confession of his complete unworthiness prepares us to marvel at his father's mercy and the grace of his welcome.

We may gain fresh amazement if we compare the story Jesus told with a somewhat similar story in the literature of Mahayana

Buddhism. In a famous "Lotus Sutra" the story is told.[1] A young man leaves his father's house and is gone for many years, "twenty or thirty or forty or fifty." His father searches for him and moves to another country, where he becomes immensely wealthy. The son, on the other hand, continues his wanderings as a despised beggar. One day the son happens to come to the town where his father lives. He does not recognize his father, but stares with curiosity at the princely magnificence of this elderly man. Fanned by attendants, the father sits on a throne under a jeweled awning, his footstool decorated in gold and silver. He is concluding business deals in gold bullion, corn, and grain with a surrounding crowd of merchants and bankers. The beggar is thoroughly alarmed. "People like me don't belong here," he thinks. "Let me get out of here before I am seized to do forced labor."

But the father has recognized his son at first sight and sends his servants after him. They bring him back, kicking and screaming in terror. Sure that he will be put to death, he faints dead away. The father sprinkles cold water on him, and tells the servants to let him go. He does not identify himself to his son, or his son to his servants. Instead, he sends servants to find him again in the slum section of the city, and to bring him back with an offer of employment. The servants disguise themselves as street people, smearing dirt on themselves and wearing rags, so as to gain the trust of this beggar. Their mission succeeds, and the poor man is set to work at the lowliest of tasks. (The estate is not equipped with septic tanks.) The father watches his son through a window as he is shoveling manure, or, rather, basketing it. He, too, smears on dirt and puts on rags so as to go and talk to his son and encourage him on the job. The son works faithfully on the grounds, but continues to live in a shack nearby. Many years later, the father expresses great appreciation for the son's faithful work; he declares that he will treat him as a son and make him his heir. The son is indifferent to all the wealth that is now declared to be his; he continues to live in his shack and work on the estate.

After some twenty years, "the householder perceives that his son

---

[1] Chapter 4 of the *Saddharma-Pundarika*, ed. F. Max Mueller, in *Sacred Books of the East*, vol. 21 (Oxford: Clarendon, 1909), 98-117.

is able to save, mature and mentally developed; that in the consciousness of his nobility he feels abashed, ashamed, disgusted, when thinking of his former poverty." Aware of his approaching death, the householder calls his relatives, officials, and neighbors, and declares before them all, "This man is my natural son, the heir of all that I possess."

The moral at the end of the story is that "as we have always observed the moral precepts under the rule of the Knower of the world, we now receive the fruit of that morality which we have formerly practised."

What is the difference between these two stories? One word describes it: *grace!* Amazing grace! Watch the father in the parable told by Jesus. Far down the road he sees that familiar figure. He sweeps up the skirt of his robe, thrusts it into his belt, and runs down the road to meet his son. He flings his arms around him, hugs him to his chest, and kisses the dusty cheeks of that swineherd. "Father," the son begins, "I have sinned against heaven and against you. I am no longer worthy to be called your son . . ."

The father will not hear more. Turning back to the house with his arm around his son, he is calling to the servants, "Quick! Bring the best robe and put it on him. Put a ring on his finger and sandals on his feet. Bring the fattened calf and kill it. Let's have a feast and celebrate. For this son of mine was dead and is alive again; he was lost and is found" (Luke 15:22-24, NIV).

So full and free is the forgiveness of the father that he will have no delay in restoring to his son the symbols of his status. The best robe is a symbol of honor; the signet ring bears the father's seal; even sandals carry meaning—servants went barefoot. And then the feast! What a welcome!

Where is the father's prudence? Didn't the younger son disgrace his name? What has the man been doing? What of those rumors? What does he expect now, more money?

No, the father does not arraign his son with questions; he welcomes him in the triumph of joy. His son was dead, and is alive; was lost, and is found. The father's joy is kindled by the fire of his love.

The Scripture often pictures the love of a father: Abraham taking his beloved son Isaac up Mount Moriah. Must he, indeed, offer him up in sacrifice there?

Old Israel had been shown the blood-stained coat of Joseph, his favorite son, and had given him up for dead, the prey of some wild beast. Then he learned that Joseph, sold as a slave by his brothers, was a prince of Egypt. He went down to Egypt and was met on the way by Joseph. His son, whom his grief had counted to be dead, was alive in his arms.

King David was a poor father, by turns too strict and too indulgent, but he loved his rebellious son Absalom desperately. When the great battle was fought between the forces of David and Absalom, the king seemed less concerned about the outcome than about the safety of his son. When the messenger of victory confirmed that Absalom was dead, David wept, "O my son Absalom! My son, my son Absalom! If only I had died instead of you—O Absalom, my son, my son!" (2 Sam. 18:33, NIV).

Yet the greatest cry of a father's love in the Old Testament comes not from David but from his God. The Lord had owned the people of Israel as his son in Egypt. His demand to Pharaoh was, "Let my son go, so he may worship me" (Ex. 4:23, NIV). The Lord guided his first-born son through the desert, as a father might teach an infant son to walk (Hos. 11:1-4). When Israel became a rebellious son, God pronounced his judgments on their apostasy. Yet from his heart of love he cried out,

> "How can I give you up, Ephraim?
>   How can I hand you over, Israel? . . .
> My heart is changed within me;
>   all my compassion is aroused" (Hos. 11:8, NIV).

THE DEMAND OF THE FATHER'S WELCOME

The scene shifts. We are out in the field as the furrows fall into shadow. The older brother is coming in from his work. As he nears the house, he listens and looks up. Yes, it's music, the music of a band playing. The house is blazing with light. There is singing, dancing; the whole hilltop is rocking. He calls to one of the hands. "What," he asks, "is going on up there?"

We have the feeling that he knows very well what is going on. There hasn't been a party like this since before his brother left home! The servant answers, "Your brother has come, and your father has killed the fattened calf because he has him back safe and sound" (Luke 15:27, NIV).

The older brother flings down his staff, folds his arms, and begins a slow burn. A celebration, indeed! He's not too surprised that the prodigal has shown up, but what has he done to deserve this? He should be flogged rather than feted! The brother is disgusted at his father's behavior. *At least he can't expect me to celebrate,* he thinks. *After all, the property has been divided, and what remains is mine: that best robe, that signet ring, and most particularly that sleek calf saved for a great feast.*

He despises the father's joy, is made furious by his grace, and resents his love for the prodigal.

The servant takes the news to the father. His older son is stalking about in the field, furiously angry, and refuses to come in to the feast. The father quickly leaves the feast; he goes down the path the second time to call his older son home. Clearly the older brother in the story images the Pharisees, Jesus' self-righteous opponents. In the preceding chapter of Luke another parable issues a stern warning to them. They are like guests who refuse an invitation to a banquet. The offended host sends his servant to bring in other guests from the streets and alleys of the town and from the highways and byways of the country. Every seat will be filled with the poor, the crippled, the blind, and the lame. There will be no room any longer for the invited guests.

The Pharisees despise the poor and disdain Christ's call to the feast of the kingdom. They are warned that others will be seated at heaven's feast, and they will find themselves forever excluded. But in this parable, Jesus still holds the door open for the Pharisees. They are standing outside, furious because Jesus is celebrating with publicans and sinners. But Jesus says the Father still comes down the path to call to them. Let them consider what it means if they reject his call, if they refuse to come in to the feast of glory.

The father pleads with his older son to come in to the banquet. He receives a bitter response: "Look! All these years I've been slaving for you and never disobeyed your orders. Yet you never gave me even a young goat so I could celebrate with my friends. But when this son of yours who has squandered your property with prostitutes comes home, you kill the fattened calf for him!" (Luke 15:29-30, NIV).

That bitter son is farther from home there in the field than the prodigal was in the pigpen. He has no love for his father. Keeping his father's orders is drudgery; working for him is slavery. His real pleasure is not with his father; like the prodigal at the beginning of the story, he would prefer celebrations with his own friends. He has no conception of his father's love—for his brother, or for him. He has no love for his brother, either. He will not call him "my brother" but only "this son of yours."

The father's rebuke is gentle: "My son, you are always with me, and everything I have is yours. But we had to celebrate and be glad, because this brother of yours was dead and is alive again; he was lost and is found" (Luke 15:31-32, NIV).

The tenderness is there. Did it mean nothing to the older son that he was ever with the father? Was his relation with his father really that of a slave? Did he begrudge a fatted calf when the whole inheritance was his? Did he care nothing that his brother was not dead but alive?

Yes, the rebuke is tender, but the demand is clear. If he is indeed a true son of the father, he must come in to the feast. He cannot remain there in the outer darkness, burning with anger and jealous rage.

Suppose the older brother had indeed known his father's heart. What would he have done? Surely he would have come running into the house when he was told that his brother had returned. Might he have done more? Well, if he had really shared his father's feelings, he, too, would have been looking for his brother. Perhaps, being already out in the field, he might have seen him first and gone running to meet him. Could he have done more?

During the war in Vietnam, Army Lieutenant Daniel Dawson's reconnaissance plane went down over the Vietcong jungle. When his brother Donald heard the report, he sold everything he had, left his wife with $20, and bought passage to Vietnam. There he equipped himself with a soldier's gear and wandered through the guerilla-controlled jungle, looking for his brother. He carried leaflets picturing the plane and describing in Vietnamese the reward for news of the missing pilot. He became known as *Anh toi phi-cong*—the brother of the pilot. A *Life* magazine reporter described his perilous search.[2]

Yes, the older brother could have done more. If he had really cared, he could have done what Donald Dawson did. He could have gone to the far country, looking for his brother. Indeed, this is not an idle suggestion, for it is at the heart of the parable. This parable is one of three that Jesus told in Luke 15, all in response to the bitter criticism of Jesus by the Pharisees and teachers of the law. Jesus was surrounded by tax collectors and sinners, eager to hear his teaching. The Pharisees muttered, "This man welcomes sinners and eats with them" (Luke 15:2, NIV).

Jesus replied with the parables of the lost sheep, the lost coin, and the lost son. Each story ends with a joyful feast to celebrate the finding of what had been lost. The shepherd calls his friends to a party because he has found his sheep. The woman invites her friends because she has found her lost coin. The father celebrates the recovery of his lost son, and calls the older brother to join in the joy. Jesus is teaching that there is joy in heaven over one sinner who repents. But he is also contrasting his ministry with the attitude of his critics. They complain because he associates with sinners. He replies that he seeks sinners because his Father does. Jesus is pictured in the shepherd, who seeks the one sheep that is lost. He is pictured, too, in the woman who sweeps her house seeking the coin that was lost. Jesus does not appear, however, in the parable of the prodigal son. Instead, he steps out of the story and puts in his place the figure of the Pharisees. The older brother is doing just what they were doing:

2 "A Haunted Man's Perilous Search," *Life*, March 12, 1965.

refusing to associate with sinners. Jesus is doing the opposite. He understands his Father's heart of mercy. He is not only willing to go in with sinners to heaven's feast; far more, he has come to look for sinners where they are. He has come to seek and to save that which is lost. He seeks out tax collectors, stopping under the sycamore-fig tree to call Zacchaeus down, and inviting himself to his house. He finds a fallen woman by a well in Samaria, and speaks forgiveness to a murderer crucified with him.

We do not understand this parable if we forget who told it, and why. Jesus Christ is our older Brother, the firstborn of the Father. He is the seeking Shepherd who goes out to find the lost; he is the Resurrection and the Life who can give life to the dead; he is the Heir of the Father's house. To him the Father can truly say, "Son, all that I have is yours." He who is the Son became a Servant that we might be made the sons and daughters of God. This parable is incomplete if we forget that our older brother is not a Pharisee but Jesus. He does not merely welcome us home as the brother did not; he comes to find us in the pigpen, puts his arms around us, and says, "Come home!"

Indeed, if we forget Jesus, we do not grasp the full measure of the Father's love. The heavenly Father is not permissive toward sin. He is a holy God; the penalty of sin must be paid. The glory of amazing grace is that Jesus can welcome sinners because he died for them. Jesus not only comes to the feast, eating with redeemed publicans and sinners; he spreads the feast, for he calls us to the table of his broken body and shed blood.

The author of Hebrews reminds us that Jesus sings God's praise in the midst of his brethren (Heb. 2:12).[3] The joy of heaven's feast is already anticipated in the fellowship of the singing Savior. Jesus knows his Father's heart, and rejoices with him. Full of joy through the Holy Spirit, Jesus said, "I praise you, Father, Lord of heaven and earth, because you have hidden these things from the wise and

---

[3] Not only is the cry of abandonment at the beginning of Psalm 22 fulfilled by Jesus, the cry of victory in verse 22 of that psalm is also his. The author of Hebrews ascribes it to him in this passage.

learned, and revealed them to little children. Yes, Father, for this was your good pleasure" (Luke 10:21, NIV).

Come home to the Father's love, to the joy of Jesus' feast. Are you a prodigal, far from the gate of heaven? Jesus now comes to lift you up. Are you a smug Pharisee, flaunting the filthy rags of your self-righteousness outside the Father's house? Hear the words of Jesus: his Father calls you to repent and come home as a little child. Or are you somehow both at once: prodigal and proud, debased but despising? No matter; cast all away and hold fast to Jesus.

Or are you a believer? Has Jesus found you like the lost sheep and borne you home on his shoulder? Then consider the demand this parable puts on you. You have tasted of heaven's grace. You know the embrace of your Father's love. You know that he rejoices over you with singing. What does heaven's joy, his joy, over lost sinners mean to you?

You say, "It means that I, too, must welcome sinners, be ready to eat with them, even as I have been brought to his table." Is that enough? The true Son, who knows his Father's heart, did not simply share with sinners his robe, his ring, his sandals. He went to find them to bring them home. Where will you look today?

"Whoever does not love does not know God, because God is love" (1 John 4:8, NIV).

4

SEE WHAT IT COSTS

(Genesis 22:1-19)

YOU PUT DOWN the fork as your phone rings: "Congratulations, Mr. and Mrs. Target! You have just been awarded an all-expense-paid cruise on the Caribbean!" Or was it $10 million that was reserved for you according to yesterday's junk mail? Do you read the fine print on those million-dollar offers? Of course not. You don't need to.

Do you think the gospel offer is like that? Check out the experience of Abraham described in Genesis 22. God had promised Abraham more than a Caribbean cruise, or even $10 million. God promised him a land, a nation, and blessing to share with all the families on the earth.

Yet some of God's promises were long in coming. Ten years after reaching Canaan, Abraham had neither a land nor a nation. In fact, his wife Sarah did not even have a son. Desperate for descendants, Sarah gave her slave Hagar to Abraham, and Ishmael was born. The Lord, however, kept promising a son to Abraham and Sarah. Fifteen years later the Lord was still promising. At the advanced ages of 100 and 90 respectively, Abraham and Sarah found this absurd. Both laughed at God's impossible promise. But Sarah laughed again; her little son was named Isaac, "He laughs." The Lord had the last laugh.

Abraham was certainly blessed: he had wealth, two sons, and open pastures. What about the fine print? The cost of blessing didn't come in fine print. It came in God's command. "Abraham," God called, "take your son, your only son, Isaac, whom you love, and go to the region of Moriah. Sacrifice him there as a burnt offering on one of the mountains I will tell you about" (Gen. 22:2, NIV).

The name "Moriah" already suggests that something will be "seen." On that mountain the cost of God's blessing will be seen. Abraham will see the cost in the experience of faith. There, too, God will show the cost that only he can meet: the cost of grace. Abraham will see that God is the Savior.

THE COST IN THE EXPERIENCE OF FAITH (MORIAH)

The Cost Is Everything: Total Commitment of Faith

THE TEST: THE OFFERING OF FAITH

The beloved son, Isaac, the heir of the promise, was to be consecrated to God. The "whole burnt offering" was a gift of consecration. Abraham was to return to God what he had received from God.

For Abraham, the cost is everything. All that God has promised walks beside him in his son Isaac. If the price is Isaac, nothing else is left. "Laughter" is gone!

At God's command, Abraham had sent Ishmael away, for he was not the son of promise. "Take your son, your *only* son, Isaac . . ." Without Isaac there is none to be heir of the land, none to found a great nation, none to be a blessing to the whole world.

God called, "Abraham!" God had given him that name: "father of a multitude." How could he be "Abraham" without Isaac? Isaac is the seal of Abraham's faith and the son of his love.

"Well," you say, "I know this is one of those Bible-preaching churches, and you did read the story out of the Bible. But that's why I have trouble believing the Bible—and especially the Old Testament. Here is a story where God commands a father to murder his son by slitting his throat. If Abraham were hauled into a court, he would say that a voice from heaven told him to do it. Do you want me to worship a God who commands human sacrifice?"

Actually this story would be as shocking to believing Israelites as it is to us today. One of the great differences between Israel and the heathen nations around them was that God forbade human sacrifice. In ancient

Canaan, Molech, the god of the Ammonites, was worshiped by offering children in the fire to him (2 Kings 23:10; Jer. 32:35; cf. 2 Kings 17:31). For that crime, capital punishment was the penalty (Lev. 18:21; 20:2-5).

Why, then, do we have this strange exception to God's law? Søren Kierkegaard, the Danish philosopher/theologian, saw it as a divine command to commit murder. He explained it as the suspension of ethical laws for a higher purpose.

What we constantly forget is the justice of God. We are outraged by the racism of men who drag a black man to a horrible death behind their truck. He had done nothing to them. Yet the penalty they face at last is not before a human court but before the judgment seat of God. Jesus taught us that God is completely holy. We like to think that we are no worse than others, but we are all worse than Jesus, the only perfectly righteous man who ever lived. He is the only One who can stand in the judgment. We have all sinned, and come short of the glory of God. There is none righteous, no not one.

God has every right to condemn sinners to death. Indeed, when God judged the land of Egypt before the Exodus, he required the life of the firstborn sons of Israel as well as of Egypt. The oldest son, as representing the family, was doomed, but the Lord provided the Passover lamb as a substitute, marked by the blood on the doorpost. Later, God continued to assert his claim on the firstborn (Ex. 13:15; Num. 8:17). The sacrifice of Isaac would have been like the later sacrifice of the Passover lamb. But the sacrifice of Isaac was not to be, for he was not a perfect offering, a lamb without spot; he could not pay the price of the sins of others. Abraham could not give the fruit of his body for the sin of his soul.

THE TEST: THE OBEDIENCE OF FAITH

God could and did require the sacrifice of Isaac, Abraham's firstborn, just as God later threatened the firstborn of all Israel along with the Egyptians in the last of the plagues he brought on Egypt.

Early the next morning, Abraham prepared for the journey. Abraham obeyed without delay, but his test was not over. It continued as he chopped the wood. There must be wood enough for the burnt offering at the distant place he had not yet seen. Every blow of his axe prepared for the stroke of his knife. Two servants would go with him. He saddled his donkey, loaded the wood on the animal, but chose no sheep from his flock. He left Beersheba with the wood, a knife, and his beloved Isaac. Then, for three days his obedience paced on while Isaac walked beside him. Northward into the hill country they went. With every sunrise, Abraham believed and obeyed.

The Cost Is Nothing: Total Trust of Faith

FAITH CLINGS TO THE SON OF THE PROMISE

At last Abraham lifted his eyes and saw the very mount the Lord had identified. This was the place; this was the time. The servants must come no further. Abraham lifted the wood from the donkey. Isaac put his arms through the ropes that held the heavy burden. He settled it on his shoulders. Abraham carried a smoldering torch. They reached the hill in Moriah and began to climb the slope.

Isaac broke the silence: "Father?" he said. "Yes, my son?" answered Abraham. Their courteous form of address was measured against eternity. "The fire and the wood are here, but where is the lamb for the burnt offering?" (Gen. 22:7, NIV).

"God will see for himself the lamb for a burnt offering, my son," answered Abraham (v. 8, literal translation). In the agony of his testing, Abraham could only cling to God. He was on the mount he had seen, the mount of God, with the son God had given. God saw him there. God would see the offering that he would provide for himself. The verb for "see" in Hebrew also means "see to" or "provide."

Abraham was not evading Isaac's question. Beyond his own knowledge, he was prophesying. Abraham would pay the price, but God's promise could not fail. Abraham had told the servants, "*We* will return to you." If need be, God would raise Isaac from the dead (Heb. 11:17-19).

FAITH RECEIVES THE REDEEMED SON

They went, both of them together, father and son, to the crest of the hill. They gathered rocks and stones to build the altar. The obedience of Abraham is matched by the faith of Isaac. He does not resist, but is led by his father as a sheep to the slaughter. He allows himself to be bound, hand and foot, and laid on the wood he has carried. Not till Abraham stretches out the knife does the Angel of the Lord call from heaven, "Abraham, Abraham . . ."

Abraham was ready to give everything in devoted obedience. Because he feared God, he would pay the price. The Angel stayed his hand. On the mount, Abraham looked up and saw a ram caught by its horns in a bush. He took the ram and offered it in the place of his Isaac. Abraham called the place "The Lord Will See (to It)."

The cost to Abraham was everything, yet as he clung to the Lord in faith, the cost was nothing. He declared that the Lord would provide, and the Lord did provide. Abraham's obedience was the obedience of faith. Isaac was given to Abraham a second time. He was his by birth and his by redemption. The offering of the sheep symbolized not only consecration but atonement in the blood of a substitute.

In the total commitment of faith the cost is everything, but in the simple trust of faith, the cost is nothing. Abraham worshiped as God renewed his covenant with him.

The demand that the Lord made of Abraham is not unthinkable. He makes that same total demand of you. Jesus asks it of everyone who would follow him. Whoever loves father, mother, son, or daughter more than the Lord is not worthy of him. Indeed, only as we are ready to receive our own death sentence and take up our cross do we receive everlasting life (Matt. 10:37-39). Much as we need the power of his grace to deny ourselves and follow him, his demand has not changed. Look at the cost: it's everything.

IN THE REALITY OF GRACE

The Grace of God's Demand

TO STRENGTHEN FAITH BY TESTING

Not only in the experience of faith, but in the reality of grace, the price of redemption is revealed. In his goodness, God sends us times that try us. While Jesus was on trial before the high priest, Peter was on trial in the priest's courtyard, before a servant girl. Jesus had prayed for Peter, that his faith would not fail. It failed. When Peter swore by God that he never knew Jesus, Jesus turned from his accusers to look at Peter. Weeping, Peter stumbled out into the night. Yet the testing did not come to destroy Peter, but to show him the cost. Later, at a resurrection breakfast by the lake Jesus restored Peter's faith.

Through Abraham's trial, his faith was confirmed, and the Lord confirmed his own promise with an oath. Indeed, the testing of Abraham was all about grace. God tested to bless. The Lord instructed Abraham's faith, even as he put it to the test.

TO INFORM FAITH BY SYMBOL: THAT ABRAHAM MIGHT SEE CHRIST'S DAY

We are given two keys to the testing of Abraham. First, we are told that he was blessed for his obedience, since it showed that he feared God. The second key is found in the name Abraham gave to the place the Lord had shown him. We know it as "Jehovah Jireh" ("Yahweh-Yireh" would be better): "The Lord Will See (to It)." When God provided the ram, he not only spared Isaac (and Abraham!) but showed Abraham that the price of redemption was greater than he could pay. The Lord himself must provide the offering that brings salvation. That provision must be made at the place God showed Abraham. The Lord thus showed Abraham that after his descendants had gone to Egypt, and had been brought back, this would be the place where the promised nation would gather to worship God.

Isaac could not be the offering; neither could the real sacrifice be a sheep. The One descended from Abraham must come, in whom all the families of the earth will be blessed. "The Lord Will Provide" promises the coming of Christ. Abraham rejoiced to see Christ's day when Isaac was born, and rejoiced again when God provided the ram as a substitute for Isaac; but Abraham looked further (John 8:56). Not Isaac but the Lamb of God was the Sacrifice that the Father would provide. Abraham the prophet spoke words that endured, words that explained Jehovah Jireh: "In the mountain of the LORD he shall be seen" (Gen. 22:14, literal translation).

Who is the "he" that shall be seen? When Hagar, pregnant with Ishmael, fled from Sarah's anger, the Angel of the Lord found her by a well, and she called the Lord *El Roi*, "The God Who Sees Me." She called the well "The Well of the Living One Who Sees Me" (see Gen. 16:13-14, ESV margin).

Hagar saw the Angel of God's presence, because the Angel first saw her. Does Abraham name the mountain the place where the *Lord* is seen? The Angel of the Lord called to Abraham from *heaven*. The Lord did not come down to the mountain to stay Abraham's hand.

Abraham had looked up to see the mountain. He said that the Lord would see to the sacrifice. Abraham looked up again and saw the ram, caught by the horns. Who then is the "he" that, in the words attributed to Abraham, shall be seen? The simplest answer is: the ram that Abraham saw. (The "he" is masculine for the ram; see "offered him up," v. 13.) In the mountain of the Lord, God's provision, the ram that God "saw to," was seen.

Well may we still hold to Abraham's word. In the mountain of the Lord, the Lamb of God will be seen. A popular chorus sings, "Jehovah Jireh, the Lord provideth for me," but misses the heart of the message. Jehovah Jireh: in the mountain of the Lord, Jesus Christ will be seen. What we see is Jesus Christ lifted up on Golgotha in that very place, the hills of Moriah.

The Grace of God's Provision: God Sees the Lamb!

GOD'S POSSIBILITY: HE MUST COME

Abraham rejoiced to see the day of Jesus Christ. He rejoiced with Isaac in his arms. He rejoiced because God had seen the Lamb, and Abraham knew that no word of promise was too wonderful for God. With the eyes of faith, Abraham too saw that another Isaac must come, the Lamb of God, the Son of God.

GOD MEETS THE COST THROUGH SUBSTITUTION: THE LORD SEES TO IT!

The cost to Abraham was everything. He must not spare his beloved son. But Isaac was spared. Yet if Isaac was spared, the Father's Beloved must be offered up. Paul tells us that the heavenly Father spared not his own Son, but delivered him up for us all (Rom. 8:32). God's revelation of the cost of redemption in the life of Abraham points us to the Lamb of God: the Lamb that God provides, that he offers for sinners. The Son paid the price on Calvary. So did the Father. In mystery beyond mystery, the eternal God was silent as the incarnate Son cried, "My God, my God, why have you forsaken me?"

Not just at the Incarnation did God give his Son. He gave him also in the darkness, in the silence, as he forsook his Beloved. God commended his own love for us, in that while we were yet sinners, Christ died for us (Rom. 5:8).

The cost to Abraham was nothing, for God provided. The cost to God was infinite. He gave everything in the gift of his beloved Son. He paid the price. Yet, for the joy that was set before him, Christ endured the cross, despising that shame, and is enthroned with the Father (Heb. 12:2). The infinite price that was paid is met only by God's infinite love—for God so loved the world that he gave his only begotten Son, that whosoever believes in him should not perish, but have everlasting life (John 3:16).

How dare we even speak of such wonders, wonders that angels cannot comprehend? But it is that love, that infinite love for us, that God pours out in our hearts (Rom. 5:5). Can we endure such love without being consumed with the fire of his presence? Only his grace can enable us to receive it. God's fine print is bright with the glory of his love, love that draws us to love him and moves us to love others.

> Thus might I hide my blushing face while his dear cross appears;
> Dissolve my heart in thankfulness, and melt mine eyes to tears.

> But drops of grief can ne'er repay the debt of love I owe;
> Here, Lord, I give myself away—'tis all that I can do.[1]

---

[1] Isaac Watts, "Alas! And Did My Savior Bleed," 1707.

5

WHEN GOD CAME DOWN

(Genesis 28:10-22)

HAVE YOU HEARD this plaintive English carol?

As Jacob with travel was weary one day,
At night on a stone for a pillow he lay;
He saw in a vision a ladder so high,
That its foot was on earth and its top in the sky.

Chorus:

Alleluia to Jesus, who died on the Tree,
And hath raised up a ladder of mercy for me,
And hath raised up a ladder of mercy for me.

The Scripture passage about Jacob's ladder is found in Genesis 28. There we find Jacob in flight from the murderous fury of his twin brother Esau. Esau, the first twin to fully emerge from the womb of Rebecca, was Isaac's firstborn. In spite of the prophecy that the older would serve the younger, Isaac prepared to give Esau the blessing of the firstborn. Under his mother's direction, Jacob deceived blind Isaac. Jacob tied goatskins on his arms and around his neck. He put on Esau's best clothes. Isaac gave him the blessing. Esau vowed to kill Jacob, waiting only for his father's death. Jacob therefore fled to his

Uncle Laban's place in Haran. In the long journey, he had stopped to sleep at a spot in the Judean hills. Using a stone to prop up his head, he was fast asleep when God appeared to him in a vision.

Jacob saw heaven opened, and a stairway linking heaven with earth. Angels were ascending and descending the stairway.

THE STAIR OF GOD: GOD'S INTERVENTION CONFIRMS HIS COVENANT

Jacob did desire to receive God's blessing. He was not, however, on a pilgrimage to seek the Lord. Rather, he was on the way to leave the land of the promise. The blessing Isaac had given him spoke of rich harvests in the land, as well as rule over peoples and his brothers. But what about this blessing if he left the land of God's promise?

Most people think of religion as man's quest for God. In reality, religions provide ways of escape from God. He may be promoted to a high God, so that tribal religion can worship spirits of trees or of leopards. He may be screened off by a ceiling of laws and ordinances so the self-righteous can earn heaven on points. God may be dissolved in the yin and yang of natural forces so that we are no longer accountable to him personally. Or he may be reduced to the divine in everything, the god-in-us of New Age spirituality.

The God of the Bible, however, is the God who seeks us. God takes the initiative. He reveals himself to Jacob. He had called to Adam and Eve in the garden, to Noah before the Flood, and to Abraham in the great city of Ur. Now he called Jacob, to give him his promise. The Lord's choice of Jacob is particularly clear since Jacob and Esau were twins, and Esau was the first to be born. The apostle Paul noted this as showing the pure grace of God's choosing (Romans 9). God does not choose the influential and the aristocrats, but the lowly and despised, not the winners, but the losers (1 Cor. 1:28). Isaac, the father of the twins, favored Esau, but the Lord chose Jacob.

In the vision God gave, Jacob saw heaven itself opened. A stairway was set on earth with the top reaching to heaven. The stairway was not a painter's ladder. Once when I was illustrating Vacation

Bible School materials, I sketched the scene with Jacob lying in the foreground and a long extension ladder reaching up to heaven. What would the top rest on? Improbably, I rested the top of the ladder against a cloud!

The Hebrew word used in Genesis 28:12 implies a stone structure like the embankment of a roadway. A stairway of that magnitude would require a huge mass of masonry to support it. We may suppose that the stairway resembled a ziggurat such as archaeologists have found in Mesopotamia.[1] Of the Tower of Babel, it is also said that builders planned it to reach to heaven (Gen. 11:4). God came down in judgment on the tower of man's pride, but in Jacob's dream God came down in grace. The angels ascending and descending on the stairway revealed open communication between heaven and earth.

The climax of the vision is that God came down the stairway to stand over Jacob. God stood not at the top of the ladder, but over Jacob. We know this from God's second appearing to Jacob at Bethel. There the words are, "God went up from him at the place where he had talked with him" (Gen. 35:13, NIV). According to the Bible text, God came down to stand beside Jacob. From the presence of the Lord on earth, angels went up to heaven and returned.

Standing by Jacob, the Lord assured Jacob of the purpose of his appearing. He is the God of the past, the future, and the present. He is Lord of the past: the God of the fathers, Abraham and Isaac. He is Lord of the future, confirming his promises: "The land on which you lie I will give to you and to your offspring. Your offspring shall be like the dust of the earth, and you shall spread abroad to the west and to the east and to the north and to the south, and in you and your offspring shall all the families of the earth be blessed." He is Lord of the present, for he says: "Behold, I am with you and will keep you wherever you go, and will bring you back to this land" (Gen. 28:13-15, ESV). God's presence beside Jacob makes trenchant his words: the land on which Jacob lies, with all its stones, bumps, and hollows, is the land God promises. It is the land on which God stands.

---

[1] André Parrot, *The Tower of Babel* (New York: Philosophical Library, 1955), 15-20.

God's promises to us are no less sure. His promises are in the fullness of the New Covenant. The Lord Jesus will be with us in the presence of his Holy Spirit. He will give us the fellowship of the saints and bond families with his covenant love. Contrary to some success gospels, however, the Lord does not promise us earthly wealth or extensive real estate. He teaches us to pray for our daily bread, not for earthly wealth. And the blessings of Jesus include persecution for his name's sake.

THE HOUSE OF GOD: GOD'S PRESENCE ACTUALIZES THE COVENANT

The house of blessing is built by God. Jacob awakens. Awed by the reality of God's presence in his vision, Jacob whispers, "Surely the LORD is in this place, and I did not know it." Fearfully he adds, "How awesome is this place! This is none other than the house of God, and this is the gate of heaven" (Gen. 28:16-17, ESV).

Although Jacob saw God in a vision, the reality of the promise leaves him in no doubt. It is this land on which he lay that is the land of the promise. He will indeed find a wife at Laban's house in Paddan-Aram. Yet the historical and geographical reality of the place bursts with the heavenly glory of the promise. Bethel, the house of God, is the gate of heaven. This stairway is not another Babel, but the house and city of God. God will indeed establish Jerusalem as his dwelling among his people. As the writer of Hebrews observed, those who, like Jacob, believed God's promise desired a better city, a heavenly one (Heb. 11:13-16). In the morning, Jacob does not view the surrounding real estate, but stands in Bethel, the house of God, the gate of heaven. Bethel stands between the curse on Babel and the blessing at Pentecost.

Jacob sets up the stone that was his pillow as a memorial to God's covenant promise. He anoints the pillar and makes a vow to the Lord. It would be demeaning to Jacob to give his vow a commercial twist. The Psalms are full of the thanksgiving and praises associated with God's hearing the vow of his people in distress (Ps. 116:13-14; 22:22;

Heb. 2:11-12). Jacob recounts the promise in his prayer and makes his vow to give a tithe as a thank offering.

THE LORD OF BETHEL

Jesus illumined the significance of this passage for us when he alluded to it in his calling of Nathanael. John records Jesus' call to his first disciples. He found Philip and said, "Follow me." Philip was from Bethsaida, a town on the lake of Galilee. Philip did follow Jesus, and found Nathanael, also from Bethsaida. Philip's words poured out: "We have found Him of whom Moses in the law and also the prophets wrote—Jesus of Nazareth, the son of Joseph" (John 1:45, NKJV).

Nathanael was not impressed. "Can anything good come out of Nazareth?" he snorted. Philip's reply has helped generations of evangelists: "Come and see" (John 1:46, NKJV).

When Jesus saw Nathanael coming, he said, "Behold, an Israelite indeed, in whom is no deceit!" (v. 47, NKJV). Jesus recognized that Jacob had practiced deceit. The name "Jacob," drawn from the word "heel" in Hebrew, describes Jacob as a "heel grabber" trying to supplant Esau, even at birth. God had given the name "Israel" to Jacob. Here was an offspring of Jacob more worthy of that name.

Nathanael was surprised. "How do You know me?" he asked Jesus. The answer Jesus gave may seem ordinary: "Before Philip called you, when you were under the fig tree, I saw you" (v. 48, ESV). But Nathanael's reaction was extraordinary, "Rabbi, you are the Son of God! You are the King of Israel!" We can only conclude that Nathanael's experience under the fig tree was of the sort known only to the Lord he worshiped. Jesus addressed this new disciple: "You will see greater things than these. . . . Truly, truly, I say to you, you will see heaven opened, and the angels of God ascending and descending on the Son of Man" (vv. 50-51, ESV). "Truly" is "amen" in Greek.

The reference of Jesus to Jacob's dream at Bethel is clear. But in what sense does Jesus apply the going and the coming of the angels to himself?

Some preachers and commentators have said that Jesus is the ladder, the stairway of Jacob's vision. It is true enough that Jesus spoke of his own descending to earth and of his ascending again to heaven (Prov. 30:4; John 3:13). But to Nathanael he spoke of the *angels* ascending and descending. The interpretation is not difficult in the light of what we have learned about Bethel. The Lord came down at Bethel. Since the Lord who came down was the Second Person of the Trinity, the person who reveals the Father, it is natural that Jesus would speak about the angels ascending from him at the bottom of the ladder, and coming down to him there. They did not ascend and descend in relation to Jacob but in relation to Jesus. Jesus here speaks of his second coming, when he will come in glory to this planet, attended by the angels of heaven.

The dispensational teaching of a secret rapture of the church has no ground in Scripture beyond a forced interpretation of "Come up here" in Revelation 4:1. There the voice like a trumpet summons John to enter in the Spirit to a heavenly scene, a part of the revelation he received on the Isle of Patmos.

The Lord who came down the stairway of Jacob's dream is the Lord who came down to be born of Mary. Here on earth he could tell Nathanael that he knew him, and had seen him under the fig tree. He could also tell him of the glory of his second coming. The angels of Jacob's dream will come with him then. They had come to the shepherds to announce his birth. They will come with him when he comes in glory.

The clear teaching of Paul in his second letter to the Thessalonians shows us what our hope is. Christ's second coming will bring relief to troubled Christians. "This will happen when the Lord Jesus is revealed from heaven in blazing fire with his powerful angels" (1:7, NIV). It is this coming that Jesus refers to in his words to Nathanael. Jesus reminds Nathanael—and us—that marvelous as it is that the Lord sees us in our times of devotion and fellowship with him, the Second Coming will be vastly more marvelous. Precious are our times under a "fig tree" when we experience the presence of the Lord, when we are aware that he sees us. Blessed is that assurance of faith as the Spirit applies that very word of Christ to our hearts. Yet we believe in hope, looking for the appearing of our great God and Savior, Jesus Christ.

As we wait for the Lord, look to him now. Jacob found a dream to be Bethel, the house of God, the gate of heaven. You have not a dream to cherish but a living Savior who speaks to you in his Word and in the preaching of it. He owns you by name in the water of baptism, and gives you the bread and the wine, the sign and seal of his passion. You need not anoint a stone as Jacob did. You may, in your devotion, anoint the Lord's anointed as Mary of Bethany did.

Repeat the gospel promise in your vow of faith. You will see Jesus when he comes with his angels. But he sees you now and comes to you—the Lord is in this place, and you did not know it! This is your Bethel, the house of God. Come home!

6

THE CHAMPION'S STRANGE
VICTORY

(Genesis 32)

TO UNDERSTAND THE thirty-second chapter of Genesis, we need to take *wrestling* more seriously. You may think I'm joking. How could anyone take wrestling seriously after watching television buffoonery? I once watched a bout won by an actor called the Hulk. I'll admit the announcer pretended to take it seriously. There may even have been people in the crowd who were bamboozled by the choreography. (They must never have watched the close-up shots on television.)

On second thought, there is a serious side to it. What if the four-hundred-pound gentleman called the Earthquake really did crash-land on an opponent's ribcage in a leap from the ringside ropes? I didn't stay tuned.

Collegiate wrestling, I hasten to add, is a genuine sport, but even that is not taken as seriously as football and basketball. Even regional finals don't begin to command the audiences that crowd sumo wrestling in Japan.

In the ancient New East, wrestling had great importance. Sumerian mythology described a fierce wrestling match between Gilgamesh, the king of Erech, and Enkidu, who then became his friend. Further, wrestling was one form of trial by combat. As David's engagement with Goliath determined a battle's outcome, so wrestling could serve as an ordeal to determine the issue of a trial.

You may recall God's dealings with the patriarch Jacob. He deceived Isaac, his blind father, and secured the blessing that Isaac would have given his twin brother Esau. Esau threatened Jacob's life, and Jacob fled to his uncle's home in Haran, far beyond the boundaries of Canaan. But before he left the land of promise, God appeared to him at Bethel, coming down the stairway in Jacob's dream to assure him that God's covenant blessing was indeed his. God would not leave him, would bring him again to the land, and would keep all his promises of blessing.

Now we find Jacob returning to Canaan at God's command. He left as a lonely exile; he returns as a wealthy herdsman with two wives, many children, and a vast caravan of camels, cattle, sheep, and goats. God has certainly blessed him in wealth. Nor is the blessing only financial. Jacob now knows that his life is in God's hands, and that God's blessing means more than cows and goats. His Uncle Laban had repeatedly deceived Jacob, switching both wives and wages, but God had overruled all his schemes by prospering the heir of his promise. Indeed, Laban too had been prospered through Jacob's service. God's word to Abraham that he would bless him and make him a blessing was being fulfilled in his grandson Jacob, in spite of the sins and failings of all concerned.

THE AGONY OF THE COMBAT

But now Jacob's faith is put to the test. After twenty years he is again approaching the land where Esau lives. Laban was a trickster; Jacob could deal with that. But Esau is a warrior. What reception can Jacob expect? With much apprehension he sends word to Esau that he has returned. He describes the prosperity the Lord has given him and seeks Esau's goodwill (Gen. 32:3-5). Anxiously Jacob looks for his messengers as his caravan moves west along the Jabbok River. At last the dust of their camels appears as they ride up from the south. Their breathless message: Esau is on the march. He is coming to meet Jacob with four hundred men. That armed brigade is obviously not a welcoming committee! The background for Jacob's combat with the angel is this threat, this crisis. Jacob's struggle with Esau had begun in his mother's womb. Now he comes to the day of reckoning. He must meet his twin, his dreaded antagonist. For twenty years that fear has never completely left him. Now it is only hours away.

At once Jacob goes into action. His great caravan is too tempting a target for Esau's troops. It must be divided. If Esau meets up with one half, the other may still escape while the plundering takes place. After the frantic confusion that produces two caravans, Jacob turns to the Lord in prayer. Listen to his words:

> O God of my father Abraham, God of my father Isaac. O LORD, who said to me, "Go back to your country and your relatives, and I will make you prosper," I am unworthy of all the kindness and faithfulness you have shown your servant. I had only my staff when I crossed this Jordan, but now I have become two groups. Save me, I pray, from the hand of my brother Esau, for I am afraid he will come and attack me, and also the mothers with their children. But you have said, "I will surely make you prosper and will make your descendants like the sand of the sea, which cannot be counted" (Gen. 32:9-12, NIV).

Jacob is no longer the independent manager of his own destiny. He is a believer: he confesses his own unworthiness, and the wonder of the Lord's grace. He looks to the Lord to deliver him from Esau's threatening advance, and he claims the Lord's promise, the promise of his blessing to Abraham.

Jacob's earnest petition does not make him passive, however, as he looks for God's blessing. Once he was a schemer; now he is a strategist. If Esau is determined to be his enemy, he is determined to be his brother's friend. If Esau would do him evil, he would do Esau good. God's covenant promise was that he should *be* a blessing. Let him be a blessing to Esau. Let him give Esau the very things Esau might be tempted to take: a magnificent gift of breeding stock. Even if you suspect Jacob of simply trying to buy Esau off, you must admit the price is generous. Would you fault Jacob for using a little psychology? If his present to Esau is the equivalent of a whole ranch, there is good reason to give Esau the opportunity to reflect on the goodwill behind it. Let the hundreds of goats be separated from the hundreds of sheep. Separate the camels, the cattle, the asses. Arrange a suitable interval between each drove. Let each drover have the same message for Esau: "These are Jacob's, a present to the lord Esau; and Jacob is coming behind us!"

Jacob thinks of one more strategy as night falls. Get both caravans north across the river Jabbok, away from the approaching Esau. At least the river can serve as a barrier. Jacob remains behind, alone. He has done all he can. Tomorrow Esau will appear.

As Jacob waited in the night, he became aware of an advancing figure. The stranger challenged him, and then suddenly grappled with him. After his initial surprise, Jacob may have looked for a quick victory. Jacob was a man of unusual strength. But this was no ordinary opponent; Jacob had met more than his match. On and on Jacob strained and gasped as the deadly bout continued through the hours of darkness. Then, as morning was near, Jacob's opponent touched the hollow of his thigh. Jacob was suddenly lame. He could only cling to this Wrestler, but now with a growing conviction. He knew his opponent for the Angel of the Lord.

To understand what this means, we must remember that Jacob's company had been met by a company of angels as they first entered the borders of the land. The place was called Mahanaim, which means "two companies." The Lord would remind Jacob that his return to the land was not something to be taken for granted. This was the land the Lord had claimed for his people, a true "Holy Land." It was not strange that there should be a guardian band of angels to be encountered at the entrance. Jacob must have been in awe of this sign of the presence of the Lord of the heavenly hosts. But now Jacob encountered, not a band of angels, but One who is more to be feared by far, the very Angel of the Lord, the appearing of his own presence.

Moses had a similar encounter with the Angel as he entered Egypt on God's mission without having circumcised his sons (Ex. 4:24; 5:3). Joshua, standing alone before Jericho after Israel had entered the land, also encountered the Captain of the Lord's host, who advanced with a drawn sword (Josh. 5:13-14).

The Lord is showing Jacob that the one he must fear to encounter is not Esau, but God himself, present in his Angel. Jacob's struggle at last is not the wrestling with Esau that began in his mother's womb. His struggle is with the Lord himself, the God of Abraham and Isaac.

Perhaps we are not ready to recognize that. The god of much popular religion is not the holy God of the Bible. He resembles more the *djinn* of Aladdin's lamp who rises at our bidding to carry out our desires. If we have no fear of God, we do not know him who is a consuming fire (Heb. 12:29). The Lord meets Jacob as a fearful Adversary.

THE WONDER OF THE VICTORY

Yet for all of the agony of Jacob's lonely combat, the heart of this story is a message of victory. Jacob wins in the victory of faith. The Angel does not overpower him until he cripples Jacob with a touch. But even then Jacob will not let go. When the Angel asks to be released as the day breaks, Jacob cries, "I will not let you go unless you bless me" (v. 26, NIV).

Jacob's faith lays hold of the Angel in sheer desperation. Here is the core of his lifelong desire for the blessing. He grasps the One who is the Giver and the Gift, the Lord of life and hope. True faith is not a flaccid acceptance of a better state of affairs. It is drawn and driven: drawn by the bursting recognition that God is real, and that he is here with me; driven by the emptiness and horror of guilt and dread apart from his blessing. Faith grips the Lord, lays hold on eternal life. What Jacob claims is God's promise; he cannot be denied, for God has bound himself.

The Lord himself pronounces Jacob the winner. His name is

"Jacob," the heel-grabber, for he has struggled with men; now his name will be Israel, for he has struggled with God, and won! (v. 28).

But if Jacob was a winner by faith, the real victory was a victory of *grace*. What a strange winner he was: "In the womb he grasped his brother's heel; as a man he struggled with God. He struggled with the angel and overcame him; he wept and begged for his favor" (Hos. 12:3-4, NIV).

Jacob certainly did not pin his opponent; his win was hardly a wrestler's victory. He won when he was helpless; he had power with God when his power was gone, and he knew it. In the morning he knew his peril better than in the night. The Lord had said, "Let me go, for it is daybreak" (Gen. 32:26, NIV). The reason, of course, is not that the Lord feared the dawn. (He was not a night spirit, as some commentators have imagined.) The danger was to Jacob: that with the light of the morning he might look upon the very face of God. It is for that reason that Jacob calls the place Peniel: the face of God. "It is because I saw God face to face, and yet my life was spared" (v. 30, NIV). He had asked the name of the angel, but the request was not appropriate. He knew the Lord, and as he received the blessing he saw in the dawning light the face of the Lord.

Here is the height of the blessing Jacob sought: to see the Lord face to face.

> "The LORD bless you and keep you;
> the LORD make his face shine upon you and be gracious to you;
> the LORD turn his face toward you and give you peace"
> (Num. 6:24-26, NIV).

Jacob at Bethel had said, "Surely the LORD is in this place and I did not know it. . . . This is none other than the house of God, and this is the gate of heaven" (Gen. 28:16-17, ESV). Now Jacob has deeper fellowship with the Lord, for he caught the vision of the glory of Christ, who is the image of God (2 Cor. 4:4). Jesus said, "He that hath seen me hath seen the Father" (John 14:9, KJV). God whose morning light shone on Jacob at Peniel has made his light to shine in our hearts to give us the light of the knowledge of his glory in the face of Christ.

Jacob, now Israel, was ready to meet Esau face to face, for he had met God face to face. Bearing God's blessing, he need fear no man.

Jacob was a winner by grace, the Lord was the Victor of grace. Christ is foreshadowed in this account, not in one role, but in two. He is the Angel of the Lord, the mysterious figure in whom God himself is present. As the Lord, he wins by losing. Had he simply touched Jacob with the finger of judgment, Jacob would have lost irretrievably. But that was not his purpose. The Lord restrains his power, withholds his judgment, to hear the cry of faith, to give himself to the grasp that holds to his promise.

Christ is also foreshadowed in Jacob, the seed of the promise, and the servant of the Lord. Christ is the true Israel, as the prophet says: "He said to me, 'You are my servant, Israel, in whom I will display my splendor'" (Isa. 49:3, NIV). Isaiah goes on to describe the suffering Servant, smitten of God and afflicted for our transgressions. Indeed, there is symbolism that points to Christ in the very stroke that Jacob received as he wrestled. The thigh in the Old Testament was a more delicate way of referring to the organ of generation. In the two other passages where Jacob's thigh is mentioned, it is his progeny who are represented by the term (Gen. 46:26; Ex. 1:5). Jacob suffers the crippling touch with reference to his progeny, to the One who will be born of his descendants, the Messiah.

Jesus Christ wrestles in the agony of Gethsemane's garden. The Father hides his face from him in the darkness of Calvary that we might see his glory. He is the Victor because he is the Victim. Dying, he lives; struck down, he is exalted over all. He will not let go till he has received the blessing. His prayer to the Father is that one day we might see his glory.

Do you ask his name? It is Immanuel, God with us. Not in the gray light of Peniel's morning do we see him, but in the disclosure of the Holy Spirit in our hearts. But the day will come when we shall see him and be like him. To commemorate Peniel, Israel's descendants did not eat of the sinew of the hip. We are called to the Lord's table to eat and drink as we remember his death for us.

Because Jesus agonized for us, we may lay hold on him. Is your faith desperate? Do you know how much you need the Lord and the blessing of his face? Do you cry out, "I will not let you go, unless you bless me"? The Lord still blesses desperate faith!

7

CAN GOD BE AMONG US?

(Exodus 34:1-9)

HOW RELIGIOUS DO you want to be? Not as religious, perhaps, as an Islamic terrorist. Most Americans manage very well to keep religion within their comfort zone. Some of your friends, however, may have just enough evangelical memories to make them vaguely uncomfortable. Perhaps that describes your own feelings right now.

There is one place where the question cannot arise, namely, standing in the presence of the Lord. Israel knew fear when the people stood before God at Mount Sinai. The Lord had delivered Israel from Egypt that he might bring them to a rendezvous at Mount Sinai. In clouds and fire God came down on the mountain. The earth shook at the presence of the Creator. The Lord spoke the words of his covenant law from the mountaintop. Terror drove the people back. Standing far off, they sent word to Moses: "You speak to us, and we will listen; but do not let God speak to us, lest we die" (Ex. 20:19, ESV).

God heard their request, and Moses went up Sinai to receive God's words. Moses was gone for more than a month, receiving God's instructions for the priesthood and for the worship and life of Israel. God gave his own plan for the tabernacle, the tent of his dwelling. The Lord's tent would be set up where the cloud of God's glory rested. The twelve tribes were then to camp around the tent of the Lord. In front of the tabernacle, on the east, the Levites would stake down their tents. The other tribes would be arranged under their tribal and family standards all around the Lord's dwelling. The Lord would dwell in the midst of his people.

CRISIS AND COMPROMISE: GOD AT A DISTANCE (EX. 33:1-3)

While Moses was gone on the mountain, the people rebelled against the Lord. They had heard the Lord's own voice forbid them to make idols. In direct disobedience, they had Aaron make a young bull of gold. To provide the precious metal, they took off their gold earrings. Moses came down the mountain with the Ten Commandments the Lord had written on tablets of stone. He heard the orgy of celebration going on below. He destroyed the idol and cried, "Who is on the LORD's side?" Only Moses' own tribe, the Levites, responded to the summons. All the other tribes were not on the Lord's side but against him!

God had said that he would destroy these rebels and make another nation of Moses' descendants. In anguish, Moses pleaded with the Lord to spare them for the sake of his own name among the nations. The Lord said that Israel had sinned deliberately. They were a "stiff-necked people" (Ex. 32:9; 33:3, 5). The term describes a horse or donkey that cannot be directed by a bridle. It takes the bit in its teeth, and plunges on in the direction it has chosen.

After Israel's rebellion with their idol, the bull of gold, God said that he would not live in their midst. It was too dangerous for them. His fearful holiness might break out to obliterate them in an instant.

God said that he would go before them as the Angel of the Presence, drive out the Canaanites, and give Israel the Promised Land. Sometimes this has been misunderstood. It has been supposed that God was substituting an angel, rather than going himself. But this is not the case, for the Angel is not just one of the hosts of heaven. The Angel of the Lord is here an appearing of the Lord himself. This Angel is just as dangerous in his fearful holiness as the Lord, for he is an appearing of the Lord. "Beware of Him and obey His voice; do not provoke Him, for He will not pardon your transgressions; for My name is in Him" (Ex. 23:21, NKJV). The Angel bears God's name; he is God the Son.

The point God is making here is that he would not go in the midst of Israel, dwelling in his tent in the center of their camp. Before the Lord gave the tabernacle plan to Moses, the place of meeting with God had been a tent pitched outside the camp. The Lord would meet with Moses at the doorway of that tent. There he would speak to Moses, "mouth to mouth."

To many suburbanites, that arrangement might seem ideal. They wouldn't like to have God too close—surely not at their office, and perhaps least of all at home. Yet they do not want to lose all touch with God. One never knows when he might be needed. Let God dwell in a church at a convenient distance, with a clergyman as his receptionist. How close would you like God to be? How close is he?

For Moses, God must be among his people, dwelling in their midst. If God would not go among them, what was the use of going to the land at all? The Israelites preferred the diet of Egypt. They remembered the fish they caught in Egypt, and the cucumbers, melons, leeks, onions, and garlic in their diet there. They tired even of manna from heaven, and were not yearning for the milk and honey of the Promised Land. The point of going to the land of Canaan was not the produce of cows and bees, it was the presence of the Lord among his people there.

The Lord would go before them, to be sure. He would drive out the Canaanites and give Israel the land. But if he were not to be among them, how would the God of Israel be different from the gods of the pagans? We dare not forget this great distinction between the Qur'an of Mohammed and the Books of Moses. Moses mourns and the people of Israel mourn when they hear that God, because of their sin, would go before them but not tent in their midst. The Allah of the Qur'an is the Great God, but he is God at a distance, the God above, not the Lord in the midst. Moses says that if God will not go in their midst, there is no point in their going. The supreme blessing of the Lord is his tent in the center of theirs: "Let them make Me a sanctuary, that I may dwell among them" (Ex. 25:8, NKJV).

The prayer of Moses to the Lord burns to the heart of fellowship with the *present* Lord. Moses cries out desperately for two blessings: first, Moses wants to know the Lord. He asks to know the name of the Angel of the Lord who will be sent with him (Ex. 33:12). Hearing that name, he will be shown the Lord's deeds—"show me now your ways" (Ex. 33:13, ESV). Second, Moses also asks that he will be shown the Lord's glory. God answers both prayers, first by proclaiming his name to Moses: "Yahweh, Yahweh El, merciful and gracious, longsuffering, and abounding in grace and truth" (Ex. 34:6, NKJV, using the Hebrew names of God). This is the name Moses heard at the burning bush. It is the name God used in declaring the Ten Commandments: "I am Yahweh your God, who brought you out of the land of Egypt, out of the house of slavery" (Ex. 20:2, ESV, using the Hebrew name of God). It is the name John uses in reference to Exodus 23, when he says, "The Word became flesh and dwelt ["tabernacled"] among us, and we have seen his glory, glory as of the only Son from the Father, full of grace and truth" (John 1:14, ESV).

Moses also saw the glory of God. The Lord hid him in a cleft of the rock and covered him with his hand until he had passed by, and Moses saw his back. When Jesus the Son, who is the glory of the Father, appeared on the Mount of Transfiguration, Moses appeared there with him. Then he could look, not at the back of God, but on the glory that shone from the face of Jesus. He saw on earth the glory of the face of God the Son, who alone can reveal the Father.

In response to the prayer of Moses, God said that he would go in the midst of his people. In his prayer of thanksgiving, Moses repeats the words God had spoken. God had said, "You are a stiff-necked people; if for a single moment I should go up among you, I would consume you" (Ex. 33:5, ESV). Moses prays, "Let the Lord go in the midst of us, for it is a stiff-necked people" (Ex. 34:9, ESV). Some translations change "for" to "although." Surely Moses can't be asking that God go in the midst *because* they are stiff-necked sinners! But Moses repeats the words of the Lord exactly. Then he adds, "and pardon our iniquity and our sin, and take us for your inheritance." The Lord must go in the midst precisely because Israel is a stiff-necked people. They need the presence of the Lord, who is full of grace and faithful to his oath-bound love.

GRACIOUS RENEWAL: GOD IN THE MIDST

God renews his covenant by giving his tabernacle to Israel. He will indeed take up residence in his own tent among his people. The plan of the tabernacle as God's dwelling has at its core the Holy of Holies, the room a perfect cube divided by a curtain from the Holy Place. God's holy dwelling needs insulation from the unholy camp of sinners around it. The whole courtyard is walled around by a curtain. Another veil separates the Holy Place from the court. Yet another veil screens the Holy of Holies, where only the high priest may enter, once a year, on the Day of Atonement.

Yet the tabernacle also symbolizes the way of approach to the Lord. The worshiper may enter the courtyard, approach the altar of burnt offering with a sacrificial animal, confess his sins with his hands upon the head of the substitute, and kill it. The rituals differ with the form of the sacrifice, but the priest ascends the huge altar to carry out the offering. The priest again purifies himself at the laver, the basin of water in front of the tabernacle. Priests also may enter the Holy Place, where they deposit and remove the bread of God's presence. Wine is also placed on that table. On the left side of the tabernacle as the priest enters, there burns the seven-branched lampstand, and in front of the veil of the Holy of Holies stands the altar of incense, symbolizing the prayers of the people of God. On the Day of Atonement, the high priest enters the Holy of Holies to sprinkle the ark of the covenant with the sacrificial blood. The ark, made of wood but covered with gold, had a lid of solid gold. On either side of the lid were cherubim of gold, their wings spread over the mercy seat, the center of the golden cover. That center was an empty throne. No image could be placed there, but not because there could be no image. God had made man in his image, but commanded that Israel make no image of him, nor bow down in worship to such an image.

Jesus Christ, the Son of God, is "the radiance of God's glory and the exact representation [image] of his being" (Heb. 1:3, NIV). The empty seat of the throne of God in the tabernacle was reserved for Jesus Christ, who is the image of God (2 Cor. 4:4). God's fierce jealousy against images was his jealous love of his only Son. Jesus could accept worship on earth, because he was one with his Father in heaven.

As the letter to the Hebrews teaches us, the worship at the tabernacle foreshadowed the true tabernacle in heaven, the pattern for the symbolism on earth that pointed to Jesus. We do now come in worship to the heavenly Holy Place. There the festival assembly of saints and angels gather where Jesus is. His blood paid the price of our sin that we might come to him in worship.

God's grace and mercy were on display in the covenant symbolism of the tabernacle and temple. Jesus Christ brings the reality of it all. The Lord said to Moses, "I will make all My goodness pass before you, and I will proclaim the name of the LORD before you. I will be gracious to whom I will be gracious, and I will have compassion on whom I will have compassion" (Ex. 33:19, NKJV). The goodness that the Lord proclaimed to Moses came in Jesus (Ex. 34:6; John 1:14). Jesus is the one with "clean hands and a pure heart" who can ascend the hill of the Lord (Psalm 24). He is also the returning Lord who calls for the gates to open at his return. Jesus ascends to heaven, his redemptive work on the cross finished, and death conquered.

Moses, in his prayer of thanksgiving for God's forgiveness, did not ask that God give Israel their inheritance in the land. He prayed that God take them as his inheritance, the treasure of his love.

The glory of the New Covenant fulfills the symbols of the Old. In Jesus we have the true tabernacle. Jesus said, "Destroy this temple, and in three days I will raise it up." He spoke of the real temple of God, his dwelling in the flesh of his incarnate Son. The name that God proclaimed, his own covenant name, is now proclaimed as the name of Jesus, the name to which every knee will bow.

Philip said to Jesus at the Last Supper, "Lord, show us the Father, and it is sufficient for us" (John 14:8, NKJV). Jesus' answer was also a rebuke, "Have I been with you so long, and yet you have not known me, Philip? He who has seen me has seen the Father, so how can you say, 'Show us the Father'?" (v. 9, NKJV). In the power of the Spirit, we do behold the glory of God in the face of Jesus (2 Cor. 3:18–4:6). In Christ we have been made God's inheritance, sealed with the Holy Spirit, marking God's possession of us, and our possession of him (Eph. 1:13-14).

Can God dwell in the midst of us? Yes! In Christ we are made temples for the dwelling of Christ (1 Cor. 6:19), and the church becomes his dwelling, for the church is the body of Christ (1 Cor. 6:15; Eph. 2:20-21). Beyond all our understanding, God not only pours out his love in our hearts but is personally present in the Spirit. Union with Christ means personal attachment and fellowship that binds the church in one in Jesus. Now and forever, to live is Christ, and to die is gain.

8

MEET THE CAPTAIN

(Joshua 5:13-15)

WHO'S IN CHARGE AT your church? Some churches are run by the pastor, others by the pastor's wife. Most Christians recognize, however, that Christ is the head of the church, and that he directs it by his Word and Spirit. In the apostolic church of the New Testament, the apostles looked to church members to choose those who would be recognized as their elders. The New Testament practice of government by elders might seem today to be a hopeless effort to run the church by a committee. Secular businesses look to strong leaders to shape the companies they direct. New Testament church order had a strong influence, however, on the democratic practices of American government.

Yet church order rests not on democratic assumptions but on the reality of Christ's rule over the church as his kingdom. Christ ascended as King of kings, and now rules over heaven and earth. In the Old Testament, Christ appeared as the Angel of the Lord to deliver his people and to bring judgment on his enemies. In a key passage in the book of Joshua, he appeared to Joshua to show his rule over Israel and the nations.

The book of Joshua introduces a new epoch in the history of God's people. After forty long years in the wilderness, a new generation of Israelites had entered at last into the land God promised them. This was seen in what they ate. In the wilderness they had survived on manna that God provided from heaven. In the land, however, they could eat grains grown in the fields around them.

The Lord marked the new era for them by miraculously halting the flow of the Jordan River so they could cross on dry ground. As the Reed Sea had opened to deliver them from Egypt, so now the Jordan was stopped in the midst of its high water. The priests stepped into the edge of the water carrying the ark of the covenant. As the flood of the Jordan stopped, they remained standing in the middle of the riverbed with the ark. Joshua commanded that twelve stones be set where the priests were standing to mark the time and place where God had brought them to the goal of the Exodus in their entrance to the land. The Reed Sea had been divided for them to go out of Egypt, and the Jordan was held back for them to come into their inheritance. Twelve stones were taken from the Jordan riverbed and piled on the Canaan shore, marking the place where the tribes of Israel had hurried up from the mounting wall of the halted Jordan.

Before fearful Canaanites on the walls of Jericho, the people of Israel entered the land. They renewed their covenant with the Lord. The men were circumcised, and the Passover was celebrated. Both of these covenant ordinances had been ignored in the wilderness by that generation. Now they marked the beginning of a new start for Israel in the land of promise. They were to be God's holy people in the Holy Land. Their task was to bring God's judgment on the Canaanites. The Canaanites sacrificed little babies to appease the gods they worshipped; their bones have been found by archaeologists under the cornerstones of Canaanite homes in Palestine. In our abortion practices as a society we should remember God's wrath against such infanticide. God's justice had determined that the cup of the iniquity of the Canaanites was full. The men of Israel were to be God's avenging angels bringing God's day of judgment to Canaan.

THE CAPTAIN IS THE LORD

The Adversary: Drawn Sword . . . Against Us!

Joshua stood near Jericho—no doubt at a prudent distance. He saw the height of the walls. God had awed the warriors inside Jericho; their hearts were melted. Joshua did not see their hearts, however, only their walls. As he stood reflecting, he was startled to see that a man was approaching him with a drawn sword. Joshua was a warrior general. He immediately moved to the attack, calling out his challenge: "Are you one of us, or for our enemies?"

"Nay," said the swordsman, "I am captain of the host of the LORD; I am now come!" (Josh. 5:14, JPS). The Lord had challenged Jacob when he returned to the land from exile in Haran. Two companies of angels met Jacob as he entered the land. The Lord then met Jacob and wrestled with him through the night. The Lord had met Moses when he returned from the desert to deliver God's people from slavery in Egypt. Facing God's threat, Moses had circumcised his sons. In the same way the Lord met Joshua as he crossed the Jordan River.

Joshua recognized the threat of God's holiness, and fell prostrate to the ground before the Captain of the armies of heaven. He recognized that the Captain of the host of heaven was none other than the Lord himself, who had come down to lead the people who bore his name.

Service of the Lord of glory must always begin in that posture. The gospel is not our product; the church is not our organization. The Lord himself comes to do what only he can do. We are servants, not entrepreneurs. A preacher of the past generation, John Clelland, used the aphorism: "On your face before God, on your feet before men."

Joshua did not boast of the size of the armies of Israel; he worshiped the Prince of the armies of heaven, the Lord Sabaoth. "But who can endure the day of his coming? Who can stand when he appears?" (Mal. 3:2, NIV).

The Captain of Our Salvation: Drawn Sword . . . for Us!

The Captain has not drawn his sword, however, to destroy Joshua and his troops. The threat of his holiness is there, but he has come against the powers of darkness, the dominion of evil. The destruction that the Lord has decreed against the Canaanites is a sign of his justice. For them the day of judgment has come. That foreshadowed the time that Jesus announced in his coming to earth: "Now is the time for judgment on this world; now the prince of this world will be driven out" (John 12:31, NIV).

The Captain comes to announce that he is the Chief of the armies of Israel as well as the armies of heaven. Joshua serves under his command. Success is promised to Joshua because the Lord will be with him as he was with Moses (Josh. 1:5, 7). Paul the apostle knows the victory of the Spirit in his missionary campaigns as well as in the lives of believers: "If God is for us, who can be against us?" (Rom. 8:31, NIV). Because Joshua—and we—fear the Lord, we need have no fear of men. Peter in his First Epistle (3:15) cites Isaiah 8:12-13. The Greek Old Testament says, "Do not fear what they fear or be terrified, but sanctify the Lord himself, and let him be your fear." Peter in his quotation replaces "himself" with "the Christ." The appearing of the Captain of the host of heaven was an appearing of the Son of God, who became incarnate when he was born of Mary.

THE CAPTAIN TAKES CHARGE

The "Dedication" of Judgment: Holy War

The Captain came to carry out the judgment long ago foretold to Abraham. Because the cup of the iniquity of the Amorites was not yet full, the judgment did not fall in the time of Abraham (Gen. 15:16). But the idolatry and sexual perversion had continued among the peoples of Canaan (Lev. 18:25-30). The time had now come for judgment. The land would "vomit out" its inhabitants. God's cup of wrath would be poured out.

This explains the ban on taking any of the booty to be found in Jericho. The whole city was put under the curse of judgment. It was *cherem,* dedicated to the Lord, and in that sense holy. No soldier in Israel was to seize spoil from Jericho, for the whole city belonged to the Lord, and was set apart for destruction by burning. Only the household of Rahab was to be spared because of the faith in the Lord that she had shown in sheltering the spies of Israel. The precious metals and vessels of bronze and iron were to be saved for the treasury of the Lord.

All this was shown by the way in which the city was taken. Israel did not reduce it by siege. Rather the priests led the people in a march around Jericho. Once each day for seven days they did it. On the seventh day they went around the city seven times, and the priests blew the trumpets. It was the sword of the Captain, not the swords of Israel that conquered Jericho. It was taken by the priests with the trumpet of God's judgment, not by the swords of the Israelite soldiers.

The Dedication of Grace: Holy War!

Here is the biblical pattern of a "holy war." Mohammed took the concept from the Old Testament. He found it in the divine commission to Israel to serve God in bringing judgment on the Canaanites. The conquest of Jericho makes evident the direct work of the Lord in claiming Jericho under the *cherem*. The bringing of this concept into the Qur'an violates the directness of God's commands to Israel, and more dreadfully, ignores the coming of Jesus and his taking command of a spiritual struggle, not an earthly army. One day every wall shall fall before the coming of the Lord. Jesus Christ has disarmed the principalities and the powers at the cross. The battle has been fought and won. Jesus the Victor ascended in triumph and now, at the right hand of God, rules all things.

The weapons of our warfare are not those of Israel of old. They are the spiritual weapons of the New Covenant: the word of God and the love of God evident in the caring and mercy of the people of God. "For the weapons of our warfare are not carnal, but mighty in God for pulling down strongholds, casting down arguments and every high thing that exalts itself against the knowledge of God, bringing every thought into captivity to the obedience of Christ" (2 Cor. 10:4-5, NKJV).

Paul writes of his ministry in words that echo the ministry of the priests capturing Jericho with the trumpets of God. He says that God has given him grace "that I might be a minister of Jesus Christ to the

Gentiles, ministering the gospel of God, that the offering of the Gentiles might be acceptable, sanctified by the Holy Spirit" (Rom. 15:15-16, NKJV). He speaks no doubt of an offering on the altar, but his words are also illumined by the capture of Jericho. Paul does reduce the walls of error and enmity to God by placarding Christ and him crucified. He blows the gospel trumpet, and the power of God gives the victory. The Lord leads him in triumph, not as the conqueror but as the captive, chained by love to the chariot of the Savior.

One day the last trumpet will sound to announce the return of the King. But the trumpet of grace is now sounding in the gospel. Jesus with the sword of his lips prepares for the day when the battle will be finished on earth, as it is in heaven. But the sword is not in the hand of the Captain. It is his spoken word that governs the storms to bring his peace. His hands do not now bear the sword, but are lifted in blessing, displaying the marks of the nails. The Captain received the spear-thrust to win his battle. Before him we fall down with Joshua and say with Thomas, "My Lord and my God!"

9

SURPRISED BY DEVOTION

(2 Samuel 23:13-17)

I'M SPEAKING TO YOU as a gathering of fans. Most of my life I was expected to be a Phillies fan. I knew that "fan" was short for fanatic, and I knew how to spell it: "Phillies Phanatic." Even the mildest fan who moves to another part of the country will have problems. I had them in Charlottesville, Virginia; in Escondido, California; and in Houston, Texas. Some fans never change, as bumper stickers prove. A country music lyric begins, "Go lay your hand on a Steelers fan, then you'll understand."

Not all fans follow sports teams. Some have an idol who gyrates in pop music. Even political leaders may invest in fans. A true fan is more than loyal, however. A true fan carries loyalty to the pitch of devotion. Lance Corporal Grable in the jungles of Vietnam showed devotion. The young marine saved his exposed buddies by charging a machine-gun nest single-handedly. He silenced it. They found nine enemy dead around the gun and Lance Corporal Grable draped over it.[1]

Woven through the story of the Bible runs the thread of loyalty carried to the pitch of devotion. Psalm 136 celebrates it: "Oh, give thanks to the LORD, for He is good! For his mercy endures forever" (NKJV). That refrain continues through the psalm. The Hebrew

---

[1] Dan Deaton, "Daniel's Den," in *New Life Lines* (New Life Presbyterian Church in America, Escondido, Calif., June, 1999).

word translated "mercy" is *chesed. Chesed* gives the bond of loyalty the depth of love. It binds those who are joined in the oath of a covenant. David and his friend Jonathan made a covenant when David had to flee from the jealous anger of Jonathan's father, King Saul. David said to Jonathan, "Do *chesed* for [me] your servant, for into a covenant of Yahweh you have brought your servant" (1 Sam. 20:8, literal translation).

Our text is all about *chesed,* even though the word does not appear. The passage is 2 Samuel 23:13-17. It is part of a review of the heroes among David's warriors. These were David's all-stars, his knights of the Round Table. Three of them had come to him when he became king of Israel as well as Judah. He was now back at the cave of Adullam, a strong point he had used in his outlaw days when he was fleeing from Saul.

The Philistines, a coastal people from whom Palestine took its name, had occupied Bethlehem, with their troops in the Valley of Rephaim, not far from Jerusalem. It was a good opportunity for the Philistines to invade, raid the crops, and drive a wedge between Israel in the north and Judah.

The three warriors of our text had left their own fields in the harvest season to serve David again, now as their king.

> Then three of the thirty chief men went down at harvest time and came to David at the cave of Adullam. And the troop of Philistines encamped in the Valley of Rephaim. David was then in the stronghold, and the garrison of the Philistines was then in Bethlehem. And David said with longing, "Oh, that someone would give me a drink of the water from the well of Bethlehem, which is by the gate!" So the three mighty men broke through the camp of the Philistines, drew water from the well of Bethlehem that was by the gate, and took it and brought it to David. Nevertheless, he would not drink it, but poured it out to the LORD. And he said, "Far be it from me, O LORD, that I should do this! Is this not the blood of the men who went in jeopardy of their lives?" Therefore he would not drink it (NKJV).

A SURPRISE FOR THE KING

One hot afternoon in the wilderness, these three fighters reported to David. A bit later, they heard David saying, "Oh, that someone would give me a drink of the water from the well of Bethlehem, which is by the gate!"

David was only musing. Thirsty people do think about water. You may remember a spring in the countryside of your past. I remember the water of my childhood in Philadelphia. That tap water comes to mind whenever I am in a swimming pool. It's the nostalgic taste of chlorine. David remembered the cool wetness of the water in Bethlehem's well. But surely David was not simply nostalgic for the town of his boyhood. He was the king of Israel, chosen by God and anointed. Yet he could not enter his hometown and drink from the well there. A leather canteen of that water would be a sign and pledge of the faithfulness of the Lord who would give to David the kingdom of God's promise.

David's comrades from the wilderness days heard what he was saying. One spoke up: "Do you hear what the chief is saying? He wants water, he does, from the well of Bethlehem!" In a few moments they had on their swords, water from the spring in their leather canteens, and an empty canteen for water from Bethlehem. The well of Bethlehem was near the gate. That would be the command center for the Philistine troops occupying Bethlehem. To get that water David's men would have to fight for it. After hiking for miles, they at last went up the hill to the town, where they were surely recognized and challenged. Perhaps two fought off Philistines while the third drew the water. Still fighting, they exited from the city and made off across the wilderness.

Did they think about the water sloshing in that special canteen on the thirsty trip back to the cave of Adullam?

Mission accomplished. They found David. "Chief, you wanted a drink of water from the well in Bethlehem. Here it is!"

David looked at them with grateful astonishment. He had given no command to them for such a mission. Water from Bethlehem was no part of their duty. Neither had David appealed to their loyalty by asking for volunteers for the mission. Their devotion was spontaneous. David's wish was their command. They had set their hearts on surprising David. They brought him water from Bethlehem!

Children, do you remember when you surprised your mother? She remembers! How about you, young man? Perhaps you failed to surprise your father on Father's Day. He has a rack of ties. I know that you wives have tried to surprise your husbands. Does he still bring a surprise for you?

People sometimes think that pastors, elders, church leaders have to be good arm-twisters to get the good work done. No, that is not true. Service in the church is surprising, a mark of willing devotion.

You see how the Lord used the devotion of the three warriors. He gave them a surprising victory. The blessing of God endued their devotion.

A SURPRISE FROM THE KING

Carefully David took the leather skin of water from the leader of the three. He unfastened the top and poured the water out on the ground. Quickly it formed a puddle, then almost as quickly it sank into the dry ground. A few Bible commentators and not a few Sunday school teachers have a problem with what David did. David poured out the water that had cost his brave men so much.

David did exactly the right thing. He poured out the water to the Lord. To David, the water from Bethlehem was the very blood of the men who got it at the risk of their lives. He could not drink it. He must give it in worship to the Lord.

David cherished the devotion of his men. He received their service in humility. He was not worthy of such devotion. How different was David from the many cult leaders who have demanded worship from their followers. There was Jim Jones, who led his followers from California to Guyana. You may remember the scene on the television camera Jones had in place. There he sat on a wooden platform, looking down on his followers. At the command of Jones his followers drank poison, and most died. We cannot forget the fiery end of David Koresh and his followers who believed him to be divine. In California the suicides of the Heaven's Gate cult were found. In Canada and France, Luc Jouret of the Order of the Solar Temple demanded the suicide of those whom he had deceived.

How different the leadership of David! He offered to the Lord the devotion his men brought to him. He received that devotion as a gift from the Lord to be treasured. Here is the key to Christian leadership. A Christian leader knows that his people are following the Lord. He gratefully receives their devotion for what it is: devotion to him for the Lord's sake. The motivation for service comes from the Lord, and it is offered to the Lord. By offering the water from Bethlehem to the Lord, David makes it a fragrant offering, pleasing to the Lord (Phil. 4:18). Through worship, David heightens the devotion of his men. Perhaps they acted mainly out of devotion to him. He had led them through so much. But David sets their service apart to the Lord.

The water from Bethlehem became a pledge of God's faithfulness to David. Yes, the Philistines were a threat to David the king of Israel, but three of his warriors could bring him water from Bethlehem. Bethlehem would again be the city of David.

THE SURPRISE OF THE ROYAL MESSIAH

The King of Our Devotion

In the last verses of 2 Samuel 23 we read the end to the list of the thirty-seven mighty warriors of David: Ira the Ithrite, Gareb the Ithrite, Uriah the Hittite. In the account in 1 Chronicles 11, the name of Uriah is in the midst of this list. Here it stands alone at the end. The name comes as a thunderbolt in the list of the heroes of David's troops.

You probably know the shocking story, or at least know of it. David, established as king in Jerusalem, rules over the dominion he has conquered. It is the spring season, when kings go out to battle. David's troops are fighting the Ammonites, besieging the city of

Rabbah. David, however, no longer feels he must lead his troops. His general Joab is a seasoned commander, well able to conquer Rabbah. David relaxes on the roof of his palace one evening, and sees a beautiful woman bathing in an adjacent garden.

David has Bathsheba, the wife of Uriah, one of his companions, brought to him. She becomes pregnant. David mounts a cover-up. Uriah is called home from service, in the hope that paternity will be thought to be his. But this devoted soldier won't go home to his wife next door, because he is on duty. He supposes that David must have a reason for summoning him and will probably send new orders to Joab. Battles are won through faithful messengers who may be trusted for instant missions with secret orders. David provides a royal dinner for Uriah; he still will not go home. David therefore sends Uriah back to Joab with his secret message. It is Uriah's death warrant. Joab, never above intrigue, arranges to have Uriah and some others slaughtered. Joab orders them to pursue right up to the city gate. When David hears from Joab that Uriah is dead, Bathsheba mourns, then David marries her. Nathan the prophet confronts David with his sin. Psalms 32 and 51 express David's repentance.

Can this be David, the king so sensitive to the devotion of his men? Could he order the murder of a soldier devoted to him to cover up his own adultery? Water from Bethlehem now has no place in David's thinking—only lust and murder, laced with horrifying hypocrisy! We may protest that David's crimes are unforgivable. Certainly David cannot be our example, far less our deliverer. Yet in mercy toward us, in *chesed* beyond understanding, the Lord has provided a king worthy of our devotion. The Lord himself comes as our Savior King.

Yes, he comes and he seeks our devotion. When Jesus healed ten lepers on his way along the border of Galilee and Samaria, he sent them to show themselves to the priests in Jerusalem that they might be pronounced clean and restored to society. They went off in faith, still lepers. But as they went they were healed. The one who was a Samaritan came back to fall at the feet of Jesus in thanksgiving. Jesus said, "Were there not ten cleansed? Where are the nine?" Jesus sought devotion. That account in Luke 17 follows a passage where Jesus describes the work of a servant. He labors in the field for his master, then comes in from that day of labor. What then? He is not off duty. He must now prepare his master's supper. The bottom line? "When you have done all those things which you are commanded, say, 'We are unprofitable servants. We have done what was our duty to do'" (Luke 17:10, NKJV).

Do you see the connection? "Where are the nine?" Jesus had not commanded the lepers to come back and thank him for healing them. Yet he expected them to come. Jesus does not ask for the reluctant obedience of doing your duty. Of course, you cannot do it in any case. What Jesus looks for is spontaneous devotion. We need to surprise God by bringing him water from Bethlehem.

"Surprise God?" you say. "Aren't you a Calvinist? You can't surprise God!"

You can try!

Our Lord Jesus receives our devotion, that something "extra" for him—our water from Bethlehem. He pours it out before his Father in heaven! Jesus is the King of our devotion.

The Devotion of Our King

We see in Jesus the *chesed* of the Servant of the Lord. His is the faithful bond of his love for the Father. The great surprise of the gospel is how he binds us to him in the commitment of abiding love. He is the anointed Warrior who breaks through the hosts of darkness to bring us water from Bethlehem. But for Jesus, it is not water at the price of blood. It is the cup of the New Covenant in his blood, blood from Calvary, shed for many for the remission of sins.

What a surprise it is to find that *chesed* is used in the Old Testament not to describe our devotion to God—the Hasidim in Judaism are the men of *chesed*, faithful love to God. No. It describes God's devotion to us! His *chesed* is forever!

In Psalm 51 David cries, "Have mercy upon me, O God, according to Your lovingkindness [*chesed*]; according to the multitude of

Your tender mercies. Blot out my transgressions. Wash me thoroughly from my iniquity, and cleanse me from my sin" (vv. 1-2, NKJV). In verse 14, David shows the force of God's *chesed* even more powerfully: "Deliver me from the guilt of bloodshed, O God, the God of my salvation, and my tongue shall sing aloud of Your righteousness" (NKJV). The last word may and should be translated "justice." Deliver me from the guilt of murder, and I will sing of your justice? How can that be? The answer is the Lord's devotion to us. He has bound himself to be our Savior, and his saving work displays the justice of his covenant-keeping devotion! He keeps his own commitment made when he set his love upon us before the world was made.

C. S. Lewis titled his autobiography *Surprised by Joy*. David closed the twenty-third Psalm, using the word *chesed:* "Surely goodness and *chesed* will pursue me all the days of my life, and I will dwell in the house of the LORD forever." Jesus brings to you the surprise of water from Bethlehem. Anoint God's anointed, and rejoice in the surprise of new life, glorious joy with him!

Yet the great surprise is not our response of devotion to him. It is the surprise of his devotion to us. The spontaneous devotion that wells up in our hearts comes as the Spirit opens our eyes to Calvary. We respond to love beyond all praising; we love him because he first—and forever—loves us!

10

THE LORD OF THE MANGER

ARE CHRISTMAS CAROLS coming to the end of their run? "Hark! The Herald Angels Sing" has done rather well since Charles Wesley wrote it in 1739, but that was long before the "Age of Aquarius" in the last century:

When the moon is in the seventh house
And Jupiter aligns with Mars
Then peace will guide the planets
And love will steer the stars
This is the dawning of the age of Aquarius . . .[1]

This "rock hymn" from the Broadway show *Hair* was more than a hit. It became sacred music, "mystic crystal revelation" for those who seek "the mind's true liberation"—in the Age of Aquarius. No doubt this astrological doggerel needs all the help it can get from both drugs and the beat; but then rock, dope, and sex are all part of Aquarian liberation. Like the Christmas carols, "Aquarius" is a hymn of salvation; it proclaims an everlasting kingdom of harmony and peace. The salvation of the new star-fated age is the ancient hope of Eastern mysticism, the transformation of human consciousness.

Just how ecstasy will bring in the political kingdom is not too clear. Will the management have to stop the world because so many young people are getting off? Dropping out and "turning on" might

---

[1] "Aquarius/Let the Sunshine In," lyrics by James Rado and Gerome Ragni, 1966.

conceivably produce an age of anarchy rather than peace. One observer of the Woodstock festival in 1969 was disturbed by the "bovine passivity" of the drugged masses. Watching those groovy pastures, he feared other shows to come when the controllers might cut the groove, package the visions, and preserve for the devout only the freedom to stay stoned.

The New Left of the 1960s worked up a formula for using mind-altering trips to serve society-altering revolution. The new mix added Freud to Marx in a Molotov cocktail aimed at all repression, psychological and social. Revolutionary action would smash personality structure and social structure together.

The Age of Aquarius quickly began to look like a bad trip. Yet it had a desperate fascination for one who saw no way out but hoped against hope. Long ago the star of Bethlehem led astrologers from the bondage of the zodiac to the worship of the infant Savior. Those who in the 60s and still today turn to the East seeking the harmony of the cosmic spheres have missed the sign of Bethlehem.

"And this shall be a sign unto you; ye shall find the babe wrapped in swaddling clothes, lying in a manger" (Luke 2:12, KJV).

Yes, we have all heard of the angel's word to the shepherds in the fields of Bethlehem. Carols are the sound of the season, amplified to fill our shopping centers. "While shepherds watched their flocks by night, all seated on the ground . . ." We all have heard, but who has listened?

"Unto you is born this day in the city of David a Saviour, which is Christ the Lord." The Lord—in a manger! Feel the shock of the shepherds. Chilling darkness in the open field, then lightning, blazing lightning that did not strike in one flash but engulfed them in blinding glory. Exposed against the stones of the pasture, they heard the announcement of the Messenger from another world.

The constriction of their fear opened to a sense of unbearable joy. "Good tidings of great joy . . . to all people . . . a Saviour, which is Christ the Lord." They had watched sheep, but now they witnessed what the prophets and sages had awaited through the centuries. The Messiah was born!

From darkness to light, from shock to bliss, from fear to joy. The armies of the Lord of hosts shout, "Glory to God in the highest!" Surely their praise must crumble every wall of oppression, every dark tower of pride and violence. The new age of God's deliverance has broken in at last.

But a greater shock is planted in the words of the angel. The sign of heaven is most unheavenly. The sign of the angels, the sign of the Lord's birth is this: "Ye shall find the babe wrapped in swaddling clothes, lying in a manger" (Luke 2:12, KJV).

The Lord of the angels—in a *manger,* the feedbin for cattle? The sign is a scandal. If this is the message, why should angels bring it? Ought not the legions of angels march on Jerusalem or Rome? What heavenly deliverance is this?

Luke is at pains to tell us how the Christ came to be born in Bethlehem. Caesar had decreed a tax registration. At Caesar's command the royal line of David must be enrolled and taxed.

What of God's promise that he would establish David's throne forever? Shall the birth of the Lion of the tribe of Judah be determined by the decree of Caesar? David himself was severely judged for daring to number God's holy people (2 Samuel 24). Shall Caesar enroll the Lord's anointed? There, on the emperor's list a name must be written down: "Jesus . . . Son of David . . . Son of God"!

The hallelujahs of the angels reflect the perspective of heaven on the strange exercise of God's rule. Long ago Elijah had been taught that lesson. Standing alone in his contest with the pagan priests of an apostate nation, he had been vindicated by fire from heaven (1 Kings 18). But *after* his triumph came despair. The pagan Jezebel was still queen; Baal was still worshiped. Elijah fled to the wilderness but was brought to the mount of God. There he found that God did not appear in the great signs of the divine presence—fire, wind, earthquake—but in the whispered voice that declared his will. Not by fire from heaven, but by his ordering of history God would destroy the worship of Baal. Elisha would be made prophet; Jehu, king; and Hazael, a Syrian king, would be raised up to be the sword of God's judgment and the instrument of his plan.

Yes, Caesar decrees an enrollment, but Caesar's decree serves God's purpose. By means of Caesar, God's providence brings Mary and Joseph to David's royal city so that the word of the Lord might be fulfilled: "But thou, Bethlehem . . . out of thee shall he come forth unto me that is to be ruler in Israel; whose goings forth have been from of old" (Mic. 5:2, KJV).

In the scandal of Christ's birth in Bethlehem, under Caesar's dominion, is hidden the purpose that the angels praise. God can withhold his judgment and still carry forward his work of salvation. His avenging angels can carry the mystery of the gospel.

For there is more to the scandal of the Lord's birth. He is laid in a manger. There is no room for him in the inn of the city of David. Incredible! Of all places—a birth in Bethlehem of one in the royal line! Of all times—when those who could trace their lineage were gathered there by Caesar's edict!

No, to Joseph's desperate efforts and Mary's silent need Bethlehem offers only the corner of a stable and a manger. With vivid irony the words of Isaiah find unimagined fulfillment: "The ox knoweth his owner, and the ass his master's crib; but Israel doth not know, my people doth not consider" (Isa. 1:3, KJV). His master's crib! Luke's word for "manger" occurs in this passage in the ancient Greek translation of Isaiah, and "master's" is literally "lord's" (*kuriou*). "The manger of the Lord": the ass knows it, but not "my people"! "He came unto his own, and his own received him not" (John 1:11, KJV).

The sign of the manger is given to *shepherds*. This too is scandal to the proud. Only on Christmas cards have shepherds and angels come to belong together. The wealthy rulers sleeping in Jerusalem— or perhaps in Bethlehem's inn—would hold shepherds in contempt. God chooses the nobodies over the somebodies; the mighty angels pass every earthly aristocracy to bring the blessing of heaven to rough men of the fields. The manger sign is no more amazing than the "stablemen" who are summoned by heaven to the manger of the Lord.

Yet they *are* summoned, and, half-blinded still, they go running and stumbling to Bethlehem. The scandal of the manger is no stone of stumbling to their faith. They will find the child there, shut out, but not abandoned; in the manger, but wrapped in swaddling clothes. No other woman attends his mother, but she lovingly cleanses and swaddles her infant son. Her devotion makes the swaddling clothes a sign, too. The shepherds find the Lord both given and received—in the manger.

There in the dark stable they see the glory of the Lord in the manger. No heavenly light glows from the stone feedbin; only a guttering oil lamp shows them the smile on the drawn face of Mary.

But the shepherds have the sign, and they see the Christ. From the fields where young David harped his praise to God they have come to bow before that Son whom David called his Lord.

"The Lord God shall give unto him the throne of his father David: and he shall reign over the house of Jacob for ever, and of his kingdom there shall be no end" (Luke 1:32-33, KJV). How these words of Gabriel must have illumined Mary's memory as the shepherds told of fresh angelic tidings. She had not been forgotten or forsaken. The Messiah . . . born of God's promise, the Messiah! The manger straw cannot hide his glory, for he has come to the poor and lowly. Again Mary may rejoice in God her Savior, who scatters the proud, puts down princes from their thrones, and exalts them of low degree (Luke 1:46-55). He is born in this stable because he is the Prince of salvation, come to shine upon "them that sit in darkness and in the shadow of death" (v. 79, KJV).

Yes, there in the manger is revealed the glory of the *Lord*. The manger is a sign of greater wonder than the birth of the Davidic King. He is the Lord's Christ (Luke 2:26), but he is more. The angel calls him "Christ, the *Lord*" (Luke 2:11). When the virgin conceives and bears a Son, "He shall be great, and shall be called the Son of the Most High" (Luke 1:32, ASV). God's ancient sign, greater than any that man might ask from the heights to the depths (Isa. 7:11, 14), has been given at last. Every sign of God's covenant promise—from the arching bow in the clouds to the sign of Jonah in the depths of death—every sign must wait for the sign of the manger. The salvation that God promises is so great that he must come himself to bring it in. David could repel the Philistines to deliver the people of God, but David's greater Son must overcome all the powers of darkness, for he must save his people from their sins. When God "lifts up his head" in victory, he ascends to his throne, where he must sit until every enemy, even death, is put under his feet (Psalm 110; 1 Cor. 15:25-26; Eph. 1:19-23).

The Lord of the angels is exalted far above them, for "he hath inherited a more excellent name than they" (Heb. 1:4, ASV). "Of the Son he saith, 'Thy throne, O God, is for ever and ever'" (Heb. 1:8, ASV).

When the infant of the manger was taken to the temple a week after his birth, devout old Simeon blessed God with the child in his arms: "For mine eyes have seen thy salvation . . . a light for revelation to the Gentiles, and the glory of thy people Israel" (Luke 2:30, 32, ASV).

Only the Lord, dwelling between the cherubim in his Holy Place, is the glory of his people Israel. When the Word became flesh and tabernacled among us, "we have seen his glory, glory as of the only Son from the Father, full of grace and truth" (John 1:14, ESV). Simeon knew that at last the glory that had appeared of old in the tabernacle had again entered the temple. The glory had come, for the Lord of glory had come. John went before him to proclaim his glory, yet he was not the Light but came to bear witness to the true Light, who was coming into the world.

In the darkness of the manger the true Light shines. "Where cattle are let loose and where sheep tread" (Isa. 7:25, ESV), there is the sign of the Lord of glory. This sign is his sign because he is Lord. No angel could take his place in the manger, for his work is beyond the power of the heavenly host. Those pure spirits, created but not born, could visit the wrath of heaven upon this rebellious planet, but they could not bring salvation to the darkness of Bethlehem.

Only glory from above all angels could make a manger the sign of salvation. The sign of the manger is God's sign of love. "Herein was the love of God manifested in us, that God hath sent his only begotten Son into the world that we might live through him" (1 John 4:9, ASV).

The glory of the manger is the glory of God's love: blinding, burning grace. The Lord himself came, the Son and Sun of love, the Giver and the Gift. Had he come in the midst of the angels to the fields of Bethlehem, then no man—shepherd, scribe, or emperor—could have stood before the glory of his face. His coming with the holy angels will yet summon the living and the dead to judgment. But had he so come to Bethlehem, to judge in righteousness, no guilty sinner could have stood before him. The angelic joy would be only the solemn triumph of heaven over a world of rebels, for all have sinned and come short of the glory of God.

Bitter men, blind to their own sins, mocked him because he did not come with angels. "Show us a sign from heaven," they said. "Come down from the cross, and we will believe!" Such men are still mocking; they boast about their own future when they will establish a justice that God cannot deliver.

But the sign of the angels points us to the glory of the manger and the cross. Heaven's high glory descends upon the hillside with the angelic host—but the word of the angel directs the shepherds away to a glory that is greater still: the Lord of the angels comes to give himself in the place of sinners. At the manger the Mighty God glorified his name; at the cross he glorified it again. When God himself, when the Son of the Highest, hallows his name in blood, then the glory of grace is lifted above the heavens.

Our generation watches space rockets burn into the empty sky; man ascends into the heavens, but he meets no one. He turns from the void without to the void within and seeks communion with the cosmos in the alchemy of the mind.

The search is vain. Suppose a man were to gain not the hallucinations of drugs or yet more dangerous delusions, but entrance into the circle of the angels of light. That happened to the shepherds; yet they tasted joy not from a mind-blowing experience with cosmic powers on the hillside but from the dark manger where they found the Lord.

The One who has ascended above all the angels is the One who first descended to the depths. "Joy to the world, the Lord has come!"

All our own seeking has been fleeing. We have not scaled the heights to find him, but he has pierced the depths to find us. The real and living God has come; the angel's gospel calls you to the manger to meet him. It is dark now, but a Light shines, the Light of the new age, the living personal Light, Jesus Christ. Don't "turn on" the weird lights of your own illusions. Turn from rebellion and illusion to love, "for God so loved the world, that he gave his only begotten Son, that whosoever believeth in him should not perish, but have everlasting life" (John 3:16, KJV).

11

JESUS PREACHES LIBERTY

(Luke 4:16-22)

INDEPENDENCE MALL IN Philadelphia is not a shopping mall but a park for the historic buildings that cradled American independence. In the center is the shrine of the Liberty Bell. The bell is more protected than it was in my boyhood, when I could trace with my finger the words around it: "Proclaim liberty throughout all the land unto all the inhabitants thereof." The text is from Leviticus 25:10 (KJV).

On one recent Fourth of July, it occurred to me that we had just celebrated the completion of the human genome project, a rough map of the codes that control our development. As editorial writers began observing, this is big stuff. On the one hand, there is the enthusiasm of those who tell us that the key to diabetes, or Alzheimer's, or forms of cancer may be found in the billions of combinations that make up our genomes. On the other hand, C. S. Lewis long ago reminded us of the threat of social engineering through chemistry. Are we to have designer children, or reinvent humanity through eugenics? Some of you will remember the novel *1984,* written when that date was decades in the future. It predicted a slave class, bred with more brawn and less brains to serve the elite. That hasn't happened, but we do have "Speakwrite" now sold as voice-recognition software.

Certainly, the issues of freedom and determinism are now on the table. Jesus preached about freedom in the synagogue of his hometown, Nazareth. His text connects with the text on the Liberty Bell.

The synagogue was surely crowded when Jesus rose up to read the Scripture. Everyone had heard of his astonishing teaching, and his equally astonishing miracles. They knew him as a carpenter, the son, they supposed, of Joseph, who also worked at that trade. They knew his brothers and sisters. A small town did not have many carpenters. Jesus may have mended their chairs, or made the new table they had ordered.

But now he appeared to be a rabbi, a teacher who had been in Judea and was now teaching in Galilee. Heads were already turned as he stood up, went forward, and received the scroll of Isaiah from its keeper.

Jesus rolled the scroll from one staff to the other until he came to the sixty-first chapter of Isaiah. He read these words: "The Spirit of the Lord is on me, because he has anointed me to preach good news to the poor. He has sent me to proclaim freedom for the prisoners and recovery of sight for the blind, to release the oppressed, to proclaim the year of the Lord's favor" (Luke 4:18-19, NIV; see Isa. 61:1-2).

The townspeople watched and waited while he rolled up the scroll, gave it back to the attendant, and sat down. Their eyes were all on him; what did they hear?

"Today," he said, "this scripture is fulfilled in your hearing."

Jesus was not merely teaching. He was issuing a proclamation. What Jesus proclaimed was the Year of Jubilee. Isaiah's prophecy spoke of the time of liberation that God required in the Old Testament law. The sacred calendar for Israel marked the seventh day as the Sabbath, the seventh year as a sabbatical year, when the land would lie fallow, and after seven sabbatical years, the Year of Jubilee.

The sounding of trumpets marked the beginning of the Year of Jubilee, the fiftieth year. To a poor man in a debtor's prison, the sound of that trumpet was the sweetest music he had ever heard. It meant that he was free. His prison time was over. He could return to his own land in Israel, the land he had forfeited through debt. It was not even to be a year of labor, for all were to eat of what the land produced of itself. That time of deliverance and restoration was to break any cycle of oppression in Israel. All debts were cancelled; the poor regained their inheritance, their families were reunited. This law was to govern debt management in Israel, because the coming of the Year of Jubilee marked the new order that was to begin (Leviticus 25; Deut. 15:1-11). The Jubilee showed that the land belonged to the Lord. The people held it from him as stewards of his gift. When Israel ignored the Sabbath years as well as the Sabbath days, the Lord judged them by sending them into exile. The land would then have its Sabbath for seventy years (2 Chron. 36:21).

If the land was Israel's inheritance in trust, then Israel was God's inheritance. The Jubilee ordinance closes with God's words: "They are My servants whom I brought out of the land of Egypt: I am the LORD your God" (Lev. 25:55, NKJV). God cares for the poor, the captive, the oppressed among his people (Deut. 15:9).

When Isaiah speaks of the year of God's favor, he is alluding to the Year of Jubilee to show that God's law contains a promise. God not only requires the day of liberation; he promises to bring that day. Because his people have been without defenders before their enemies, and have no one to lead or deliver them, God says that he will come to deliver them himself. He will put on his helmet of salvation and his breastplate of justice, and come to save them (Isa. 59:15b-17). The need of the people of God is so desperate that only he can deliver them. In the exile, Ezekiel the prophet saw the people spread out in a valley. Their situation could not have been more hopeless. To begin with, they were all dead. Their bodies were long decomposed, their bones dry and scattered. "Son of man, can these bones live?" the Lord asked his prophet. "Lord, you know," was his amazing answer.

Further, the promises of God are so great that only he can deliver on them. God promises not only restoration but renewal. When Ezekiel prophesied, the bones came together, and were covered with flesh. God's power can raise the dead and fill them with the new life of the Spirit. The greatest promise is theirs. He will be their God (Lev. 25:38).

Jesus, however, did not just teach about the meaning of the Jubilee as law and promise. His message was a trumpet call: "Today this scripture is fulfilled in your hearing." Luke does not have to elaborate on his message. God had required the shadows of the Jubilee festival. God had promised the last great Jubilee when he would come to bring deliverance and restoration. What Jesus says is that the time has come because he has come. His lips are the trumpet call. The year of God's favor, of his saving blessing, of his kingdom promise is announced, not on Mount Zion, but in Nazareth, where Jesus was brought up. The curious Nazarenes wanted to see miracles; they did not know that what they heard was a miracle. There stood the Lord among them, telling them that his new order had begun.

Jesus was the Anointed Preacher, the Messenger of Jubilee, filled with the Spirit to speak words of grace (Luke 4:22). His declaration was with authority. He who was born of the Spirit in the womb of the virgin, was anointed with the Spirit coming as a dove to rest on him. In the power of the Spirit he wore the helmet of salvation and the breastplate of justice to engage Satan in the wilderness. He is the shoot from the stump of David's line. The Spirit of the Lord rests on him. He is the Wonderful Counselor, the Mighty God, the Everlasting Father, the Prince of Peace.

Do these great names for Jesus seem remote from your experience? Or have they faded in your life from when you first heard them—in Handel's *Messiah,* perhaps?

Then listen, hear the Word of the Lord as the people of Nazareth would not. Jesus not only announced the Jubilee, he accomplished it. The liberty that he read about from the Isaiah scroll is the liberty that he gained for you. He did that as the Servant of God in his passion, and as the Son of God in his power. In his wisdom he did not finish reading the passage in Isaiah: "to proclaim the year of the LORD's favor and the day of vengeance of our God" (Isa. 61:2, NIV). Jesus did not say that the day of judgment was about to begin. John the Baptist did not understand that omission. Later, when John was put in Herod's prison, he sent his disciples to ask Jesus, "Are you the one who is to come, or shall we look for another?" (Matt. 11:3, ESV). These shocking words show that John could not understand why Jesus was withholding judgment. Since Jesus could cast out demons and raise the dead, why did he not judge the wickedness of Herod? John was in prison because he had denounced that wickedness. John had preached that the axe of judgment was lying at the root of every tree of wickedness. Why did Jesus not pick up that axe and destroy Herod? Jesus could only show John's disciples his miracles as signs that he was the One to come, and tell John not to be offended in him.

The people of Nazareth were offended in Jesus. Who did he think he was? Didn't they know his family? They knew his mother, his brothers and sisters. Who was he to announce the coming of the Jubilee, and claim to fulfill it? In a curious way, have you evaded the claim of Jesus because you think you know all about him?

Don't take Jesus for granted. He has not yet come as he will. We wait for God's "Son from heaven, whom he raised from the dead— Jesus, who rescues us from the coming wrath" (1 Thess. 1:10, NIV). The mercy of Jesus waits for you today. Do not ignore his call to you.

His mercy waits, but his deliverance is finished. The Jubilee trumpet was blown on the Day of Atonement, when the blood of the sacrifice was sprinkled on the mercy seat, the golden lid of the ark of the covenant that represented the throne of God.

Jesus read from Isaiah 61. That prophecy proclaims the result of the work of the suffering Servant described in Isaiah (53:5-6). "But he was pierced for our transgressions, he was crushed for our iniquities; the punishment that brought us peace was upon him, and by his wounds we are healed. We all, like sheep, have gone astray, each of us has turned to his own way; and the LORD has laid on him the iniquity of us all" (NIV).

Jesus did not come to bring the judgment, because he came to *bear* the judgment. He bore our sins in his own body on the cross. His suffering in our place sets us free. Justice has been done, and his power liberates us. Jesus showed that when he went on from Nazareth to Capernaum, and there delivered a man from demon possession. There, too, he healed the mother-in-law of his disciple Peter, and she could help in preparing dinner for Jesus and his disciples. Jesus delivered and he also restored: sight to the blind, liberty to the crushed. He calls us to show our love for him in deeds of mercy to the poor and afflicted.

Jesus delivers and restores. Can you begin to grasp what that may mean in your own life? The secret of it all is that Jesus receives you personally. Jesus was baptized for you. He did not need baptism to symbolize the washing away of his sins, for he had no sin. John protested that he should not be baptizing Jesus, but Jesus insisted—to fulfill all righteousness. In his baptism he was determined to be one with you. Do you see what that means for you? The Father said, "This is my Beloved Son, my chosen." Because Jesus was united with you, you by faith are united with him. What the Father said to Jesus he says to you. He calls you his Beloved. You are chosen in Christ before the creation of the world (Eph. 1:4). Believers are sons of God because they are united with the Son of God. The Spirit of God rests on you, the seal of the presence of the Father and the Son.

You are therefore free of condemnation. Where the Spirit of the Lord is, there is freedom. You are joined in the community of his church, and made his witness in the world, that you should show forth the praises of him who called you out of darkness into his marvelous light.

Yes, in your genes there are latent characteristics, but they are limitations only to those who do not know their Creator. What is true of Jesus is also true of you.

"Before I was born the LORD called me; from my birth he has made mention of my name. . . . He said to me, 'You are my servant, Israel, in whom I will display my splendor'" (Isa. 49:1, 3, NIV). Yes, those words describe Jesus. Our Lord is God's Servant. He is the true Israel in whom God's glory is revealed. But you are made and remade for splendor. Joined to Christ, you are free to display his glory in your own calling, the service that is perfect freedom.

You need not wait; indeed, you dare not wait. The Jubilee has begun, and Jesus is already our ascended Lord. Call on him today. Better, call on him right now, and begin on earth to taste of the Spirit of Jesus from heaven.

12

THE CRY OF THE
GOD-FORSAKEN SAVIOR

(Psalm 22:1)

SPIKED TO A CROSS BEAM on a hilltop, he cries, "My God, my God, why have you forsaken me?" From the prisons and torture chambers of human savagery, victims still scream. Yet Jesus on the cross was not a victim. His lifting up on the cross was part of that lifting up by which he would draw all men to him. His cry came not from the pain of the spikes, nor from the crushing pressure on his chest, but from the agony of his soul.

His heavenly Father forsook Jesus on the cross. God does sometimes forsake sinners, giving them up to their rebellion, lust, and pride. In the folly of their delusion, they do not know the joy they have lost or the hell they have gained. But the cry of Jesus was the agony that bore the curse for us.

A CRY FROM THE DEPTHS

A Cry of Anguish

The cry from the cross was a cry from the depths. The twenty-second Psalm is a psalm of the lament of an individual. David was the author of many of these psalms. In his years in the wilderness, pursued by the jealous King Saul, David called on the Lord for deliverance. Later, surrounded by hostile kingdoms, David continued to seek the presence of the Lord, his refuge, his shield, his strength. He claimed the promise that the Lord would never leave him nor forsake him. In Psalm 22, David alternates the description of his suffering with confessions of trust in Yahweh.

The vivid figures of his suffering that David used we now see to be prophetic of the agonies of crucifixion—the thirst of the Crucified, the piercing of his hands and feet, the shame of his nakedness, and the gambling of the soldiers for his clothing. His thirst is the very dust of death.

A Cry of Abandonment

Mockers of the suffering King ridicule his claims. Let God save him, if indeed God delights in him as his chosen (Ps. 22:6-8; Matt. 27:39-44). They surround the Sufferer like savage bulls, wild oxen, dogs, or lions. In their jeering at the Crucified, we see the malice of the prince of darkness. Yet the taunt, "He saved others, himself he cannot save," is gospel truth (Matt. 27:42). Because he came to save others, he would not save himself. There was no other way, as Jesus knew in Gethsemane.

In the crush of persecutors his helpers are gone. "My friends and companions stand aloof from my plague, and my nearest kin stand far off" (Ps. 38:11, ESV; 88:8). "And all his acquaintances and the women who had followed him from Galilee stood at a distance watching these things" (Luke 23:49, ESV). Yet the cry of Jesus does not lament the absence of his friends, but the absence of his Father. His Helper is gone! God had promised never to forsake his own: "Call to me and I will answer you" (Jer. 33:3, ESV). The saving power of God's right hand was never shortened so that he could not save (Isa. 59:1). Yet his Son now looks to him in vain.

Gone was the comfort of God's presence. David had sung, "Even though I walk through the valley of the shadow of death, I will fear no evil, for you are with me; your rod and your staff, they comfort me" (Ps. 23:4, ESV). Now, on the cross, the Forsaken One cries, "Why are you so far from saving me?" Jesus calls for deliverance as the sun goes dark and the earth shakes.

A Cry of Guilt-Bearing

The *agony* of the Crucified is pictured in Psalm 22; the *meaning* of his death is prophesied in the songs of the Servant in Isaiah. The Servant "shall be high and lifted up, and shall be exalted" (Isa. 52:13, ESV). Yet the next verse strikes a blow: "His appearance was so marred, beyond human semblance, and his form beyond that of the children of mankind." The exalted royal Servant, whose glory strikes the kings of the earth with amazement and awe, is the One who appears inhuman in disfigurement, crushed and broken as the Sin-Bearer. Men hide their faces at the horror of his mutilation. Yet his affliction is far more than physical, for "Surely he has borne our griefs and carried our sorrows. . . . he was wounded for our transgressions; he was crushed for our iniquities; upon him was the chastisement that brought us peace, and with his stripes we are healed. . . . The LORD has laid on him the iniquity of us all" (Isa. 53:4-6, ESV).

The apostle Peter summarizes this passage in his First Epistle. He reminds us, "He himself bore our sins in his body on the tree, that we might die to sin and live to righteousness. By his wounds you have been healed" (1 Pet. 2:24, ESV). On the cross, Christ bore our damnation. His abandonment by the Father was the Father's gift of his Son to endure the separation from the Father that is the doom of our iniquity. On the cross Jesus was alone, hearing mockery from the lips of those in the darkness, lips mouthing the fiendish claim of Satan's hate. Yet Satan's triumph was *his* doom. The price paid at Calvary was the infinite price of God's own Son. Jesus could say to the dying thief, "Today you will be with me in paradise." That vast number given by the Father to the Son, those for whom Jesus prayed, were redeemed by his death. His death was sufficient for all, but it sealed heaven for those given him by the Father. Jesus would lose none, apart from Judas, that the Scripture might be fulfilled.

A CRY TO THE HEIGHTS: A CRY OF TRUST

The Question Beyond Despair: Why?

Jesus cried from the cross out of the depth of the damnation he endured for us. Yet his cry was one of trust. His *why* reflected the mystery of his suffering and the mystery of evil. When Jesus had approached the tomb of Lazarus, he was stirred to anger, not sorrow, at the grief of Mary, the sister of Lazarus.

When Gentiles had come seeking Jesus, he knew that the time of his sacrifice was near. In the shadow of the cross, he cried that his soul was troubled (John 12:20-27). Yet he could not pray for the hour not to come, for he came for that very hour. God promised not to forsake those who put their trust in him. Israel forsook God and broke his covenant. God said that he would forsake them (Deut. 31:16-17). But on the cross, God the Father forsook the One who never forsook him. In the mystery of the Father's will, hell was the doom of the Holy One. On the cross, Jesus did not cry, "My Father!" but "My God!"

How far short our "Why?" falls when measured by the "Why?" of Christ! We say "Why?" in rebellion. "God is not just. This should not happen to me!" Our pride is offended. We turn the tables, calling God to account, when he is calling us to account. Our *whys* protest God's providence. We do not understand. We thought that we were serving the Lord with a pure heart, and now this! Why has the Lord allowed this suffering to overtake us at this time?

Bring all your black doubts, tormented imaginations, stifled dread to Calvary! Take your "Why?" to Jesus, and hear him speak from the cross!

The Answer Beyond Hope

Jesus' very question contains God's answer, an answer beyond hope. "*Eloi, Eloi,*" cries Jesus. Not just "God," but "*My* God." Jesus glorified God's name at the cross. When, with the cross in view, he had prayed, "Father, glorify your name," the Father answered him from heaven. "I have glorified it, and I will glorify it again" (John 12:28, ESV).

God's name was glorified, for his justice was satisfied. Christ's death was the "death of death and hell's destruction"[1] for sinners he came to save. He died as their substitute. He was the Sin-Bearer. God's love triumphed over the vileness, pride, and guilt of human sin. The love of the Father paid the price, for in the darkness the Father gave his Eternal Son in his human nature. We rightly say that, but to understand it goes beyond the thought of men or angels. The vow that God took on himself was kept on Golgotha. Abraham spared Isaac on the altar, but the Father did not spare his only Son. The Rock was struck to open the fountain of life. God showed his love for us, in that while we were still sinners, Christ died for us.

The last verse of Psalm 22 answers the first. "He has done it!" (ESV). God so loved that he gave! There is the measure of the heart of God!

---

[1] William Williams, "Guide Me, O Thou Great Jehovah," 1745.

13

OUR INTERNATIONAL ANTHEM[1]

(Psalm 96:3)

"LADIES AND GENTLEMEN, our national anthem!"

Network television zooms in on the pop singer crooning about the dawn's early light, under the artificial noon of the stadium arcs. Another camera picks up assorted embarrassed athletes standing more or less at attention. The baseball greats of the Red machine shift their wads of chewing tobacco—or is it bubble gum? There is Pete Rose, actually *singing* the national anthem. Then the whole stadium cheers. Patriotic fervor? No, the game is about to start.

It is my privilege to announce our *international* anthem. No one has asked me to sing it—for some reason, no one has ever asked me to sing anything—but I have been asked to present it. It is not the "Internationale" of world communism. It is the doxology of the new mankind. One day the redeemed from every tribe, tongue, people, and nation will sing the song of Moses and the Lamb on the other shore of the sea of fire (Rev. 15:2-3). But God calls us to sing it today: "Declare his glory among the nations, His wonders among all peoples" (Ps. 96:3, NKJV).

The anthem of missions does better than make the all-time top

---

[1] This chapter was originally published as "Declare His Glory Among the Nations," by Edmund P. Clowney. Taken from *Declare His Glory Among the Nations,* edited by David M. Howard. © 1977 InterVarsity Christian Fellowship/USA. Used by permission of InterVarsity Press, P.O. Box 1400, Downers Grove, IL 60515. www.ivpress.com. The message was given at InterVarsity's Urbana Conference in 1976.

ten. Here is heaven's "Hallelujah Chorus," number one in eternity. Maybe you came to God singing "Just as I Am," but you are sent to the nations singing "How Great Thou Art!"

What does it mean to declare the glory of God? From the two great themes of the Psalms we find the two stanzas of our international anthem: praise God for what he has done; praise God for who he is. To declare God's glory among the nations we number his marvelous works (Ps. 96:3) and we bless his name (v. 2).

STANZA ONE: SING HIS MIGHTY WORKS!

The Lord is King! The cymbals clash, the people shout God's holy name. Psalm 96 is a psalm of *acclamation*. The ancient Babylonians enthroned their god Marduk in a ritual New Year festival. But Israel shouts for him whose throne is established forever. One living God is the King of the nations because he is the God of creation. "All the gods of the peoples are idols, but the LORD made the heavens" (v. 5, NKJV). Israel calls the nations not to better worship of the gods, but to worship a better God—indeed the only God.

Ancient heathen hymns are full of descriptive praise telling the gods how great they are[2]; a man with a large pantheon, like a man with a large harem, must be unusually convincing to the immediate object of his devotion. But the Psalms of Israel ring with declarative praise, glorifying God for what he has *done,* beginning with his works of creation.

The apostle Paul stands on the rocky knoll of the Aeropagus just beneath the Acropolis of Athens. In the shadow of the world's most beautiful temples he declares, "The God that made the world and all things therein, he being Lord of heaven and earth, dwelleth not in temples made with hands . . ." (Acts 17:24, ASV). Not Zeus or Athena, but the God unknown to Greek wisdom is the Creator and the Judge of the world.

"Praise him, ye heavens of heavens, and ye waters that are above the heavens. Let them praise the name of the LORD; for he com-

---

[2] Claus Westermann, *The Praise of God in the Psalms* (Richmond, Va.: John Knox, 1965), 38-42.

manded, and they were created. . . . Fire and hail, snow and vapor; stormy wind, fulfilling his word; mountains and all hills, fruitful trees and all cedars" (Ps. 148:4-5, 8-9, ASV). Descend with Jacques Cousteau to behold God's wonders in the deep; ascend with the astronauts and read the Genesis account in space. "O LORD, our Lord, how excellent is thy name in all the earth, who hast set thy glory above the heavens" (Ps. 8:1, KJV).

Job's complaints were turned to adoration when God challenged him to consider the constellation of Orion, the thighbone of the hippopotamus, and the scales of the crocodile (Job 40–41). But you do not need a telescope, a microscope, or even a trip to the zoo to find wonders from God's hand. Here you are, men and women, made in God's image. Before the vastness of the galaxies the psalmist may cry, "What is man, that thou art mindful of him?" (Ps. 8:4, KJV). But you are called to rule the earth; more than that, you are called to walk on earth with God your Maker. How beautifully the Bible describes the creation of man—God quickens the work of his fingers with the breath of his lips. The breath you draw to shout God's praise is the gift of him who made you for himself.

We need not hold our God-given breath while a landing craft on Mars turns over rocks looking for life. We know that we are not alone in the universe, and we have better companionship than anything that can crawl from under Martian rocks. "Know ye that the LORD he is God: it is he that hath made us, and not we ourselves" (Ps. 100:3, KJV). "Come, let us worship and bow down; let us kneel before the LORD our Maker" (Ps. 95:6, KJV).

Praise is more than our duty; it is our *humanity.* Men have climbed Everest, they tell us, because the mountain is *there.* How much more must we climb God's holy hill in worship because God is *there*, revealing his glory to man made in his image!

The God of the Psalms is *ruler* as well as Creator. When the psalmist tells us that the world is established, that it cannot be moved (Ps. 96:10), he is celebrating God's works in controlling both nature and history. The nations rage, but God has only to speak and the earth melts (Ps. 46:6).

Every proud empire stands under God's judgment. Long after World War II there still stood in a West Berlin park a memorial from World War I. A bronze sculpture showed two German soldiers carrying a wounded comrade from the field of battle. The fury of the battle for Berlin in the second war had pocked the base of the statue with bullet marks. A more bizarre freak occurrence of battle made the sculpture a grotesque monument to the absurd: a shell had carried away the bronze head of the wounded soldier. The two heroes now labored to carry off a headless corpse. What a macabre monument to the ruin that Hitler's demonic genius brought upon Germany! As every earthly empire must, Hitler's thousand-year Reich came under the judgment of Almighty God.

God breaks the arrows of the bow (Ps. 76:3), burns the chariot in fire, and is terrible to the kings of the earth (Ps. 76:12). God is terrible in justice. He hears the cry of the poor and oppressed from the barrios of earth; not one act of exploitation will go unavenged. "Vengeance is mine; I will repay, saith the Lord" (Rom. 12:19, KJV; Deut. 32:35). God's justice delayed is not justice denied. God is *coming* to judge the earth. The last judgment is not convened by a military tribunal protecting privilege or by a people's court seeking revolutionary vengeance; it is summoned by the righteous King of all the nations.

Declare the glory of the coming Judge. God's song for the nations thunders from the storm-cloud of God's wrath against wickedness. Paul preached the day of judgment to Athenian idolaters; missionary messengers must today be prophets of God's righteousness, calling the nations to repentance.

But is the anthem of missions accompanied only by the crescendo of God's trumpet, summoning the nations to God's work of judgment? No, the psalmist hails God not only as the King of the nations but as Savior: "Sing unto the LORD, bless his name; show forth his salvation from day to day" (Ps. 96:2, KJV). If God came only in wrath, who could stand before his holiness? We may call down fire from heaven upon the sins of others, but how shall we escape when our own sins are judged?

Praise God, the cloud of glory is bright with mercy. Declare the glory of his saving acts—the glory of the fire that filled the bush in the desert but did not consume it, the glory of the "I AM" God who called to Moses from the fire to promise deliverance to his people groaning under the lash.

Declare his glory—the Psalms sing of God's mighty acts in Egypt; they echo the song of Moses on the shore of the Reed Sea: "I will sing unto the LORD, for he hath triumphed gloriously: the horse and his rider hath he thrown into the sea. The LORD is my strength and song, and he is become my salvation" (Ex. 15:1-2, KJV).

What glory Israel can sing! Pinned against the sea by the war chariots of Pharaoh's striking force, the people saw the cloud of God's glory become a wall of darkness and fire to restrain the enemy, and then a pillar of cloud to lead them through the parted sea (Pss. 77–78; 105–106). The Psalms sing, too, of God's wonders in the desert when he led his flock like a Shepherd, fed them with bread from heaven, and satisfied their thirst with water from the rock (Pss. 78; 105–106; Neh. 9:17). The God of creation is the Lord of salvation.

But God's glory cloud did not just lead his people out of slavery. He brought them out that he might bring them in. At Sinai God said, "Ye have seen . . . how I bare you on eagles' wings, and brought you unto myself" (Ex. 19:4, KJV).

"Unto myself!" On Sinai God came down in glory to establish his covenant with his redeemed people, to speak to them the words of his law. Through the mediation of Moses, God gave Israel his law and his sanctuary. The glory that dazzled their eyes as it was reflected from the face of Moses filled the tabernacle, for God came down to dwell among his people.

God's exodus deliverance became a triumphal entry. The glory of God led his people into the Promised Land and up the height of his holy hill. There his glory filled his dwelling place in Zion. Indeed, this is the picture in Psalm 96. The Chronicler quotes the psalm in the context of King David's establishment of the service of praise after the ark of the Lord had been brought to Jerusalem (1 Chron. 16:23-33).

"God is gone up with a shout, the LORD with the sound of a trumpet" (Ps. 47:5, KJV). "Lift up your heads, O ye gates; even lift them up, ye everlasting doors; and the King of glory shall come in" (Ps. 24:9, KJV).

The God of salvation is King in Zion. His trumpet sounds, summoning the nations to worship at his holy hill. Israel's shout of praise echoes to the islands of the sea.

For a moment God's glory did rest on Zion. Solomon's temple was filled with glory. The kings of the earth and the queen of the South came to Jerusalem to hear the wisdom of God's anointed, to see the blessing God had poured out on his chosen people (1 Kings 4:34; 10:6-9).

But Solomon turned from wisdom to folly, the kingdom was soon divided, and God's blessing was turned to judgment. Where the cloud of glory had rested on God's house, there arose the smoke of burning as invading Gentiles put the torch to the cedar of the temple.

Is Psalm 96, then, part of an ancient hymnbook to be found only under the charred remains of a gutted temple? No, Psalm 96 is the Word of God, the saving God who remembers his promise to Abraham and the nations. Psalm 96 is a *new* song: God's mighty deeds of the past will be fulfilled in his great deliverance in the future.

Isaiah takes up the song of Moses to celebrate a second exodus: "The LORD, even the LORD, is my strength and song; and he is become my salvation" (Isa. 12:2, ASV; Ex. 15:2). But what hope of glory can remain when Jerusalem is ruined and God's people are scattered among the nations? Ezekiel sees the glory of God departing from the temple; he sees the people of God—dead and decomposed, dry bones scattered in the valley. "Son of man, can these bones live?" (Ezek. 37:3, KJV).

Only One can bring life from death and glory from destruction. God himself must come in the power of his Spirit and the wonder of his presence. Man's plight is too hopeless for any other deliverer, and God's own promises are too great for any lesser fulfillment.

The new song is an advent hymn: "Prepare ye the way of the

LORD, make straight in the desert a highway for our God. . . . The glory of the LORD shall be revealed, and all flesh shall see it together" (Isa. 40:3, 5, KJV).

Wonder of wonders, God will come not just to save his people from their captors but to save them from their sins. God will come not only as the King of glory but as the Lord our righteousness (Jer. 33:16). Not only will he tread the enemy underfoot; "he will tread our iniquities under foot; and thou wilt cast all their sins into the depths of the sea" (Mic. 7:19, ASV).

The Lord will come and the Servant will come. He is the Branch of Righteousness (Jer. 33:15), the Son of David, called to sit at God's right hand (Ps. 110:1). He is the root of Jesse. "Unto him shall the nations seek" (Isa. 11:10, ASV). When God's judgment hews down the cedar of Israel's pride, he does not utterly destroy his people. No, there is a remnant; a tiny shoot springs up from the stump of the fallen tree. Here is the Christmas tree of the prophet. God's shoot, God's Branch, grows to become a great mast on the mountain, a standard to which the nations are drawn.

That shoot from the root of David is the Lord's Messiah. By him and to him the nations are gathered. But the mystery of God's salvation lies in the Messiah's work. To redeem his people, God must blot out as a thick cloud their transgressions and sins (Isa. 44:22). The kings of the earth are astonished when they see the face of God's Servant. Torn and scarred, he is inhuman in the anguish of his suffering (Isa. 52:14). He is despised as a shoot out of dry ground. Yet "surely he hath borne our griefs, and carried our sorrows. . . . He was wounded for our transgressions, he was bruised for our iniquities. . . . Thou shalt make his soul an offering for sin. . . . He poured out his soul unto death, and was numbered with the transgressors: yet he bare the sin of many, and made intercession for the transgressors" (Isa. 53:4-5, 10, 12, ASV).

Now we see him who is raised as an ensign above the nations— he is lifted on a cross. "And I, if I be lifted up from the earth," said Jesus, "will draw all men unto myself" (John 12:32, ASV). John explains, "But this he said, signifying by what manner of death he should die" (v. 33, ASV).

"Declare his glory among the nations." What wonders are the nations to hear? That the God of glory, the King of the nations has come to save. The Lord has come as the Servant. Heaven's glory drives darkness from the fields of Bethlehem. An angel announces, "Unto you is born this day in the city of David a Saviour, which is Christ the Lord" (Luke 2:11, KJV). But shepherds, not the nations, see the glory, and the sign they receive is a child lying in the feedbin of a stable!

What wonder silences us before the mystery of God's coming in Jesus Christ! Yes, the glory has come, for he has come. "Arise, shine; for thy light is come, and the glory of the LORD is risen upon thee. . . . Nations shall come to thy light, and kings to the brightness of thy rising" (Isa. 60:1-3, ASV). The magi follow his star from the East and worship him; old Simeon holds the infant Jesus and blesses God for the salvation "prepared before . . . all peoples; a light for revelation to the Gentiles, and the glory of thy people Israel" (Luke 2:31-32, ASV).

Indeed both John the Baptist and Jesus come preaching the kingdom of God: the message of the coming of God the King taken from the royal psalms and the good news proclaimed by Isaiah. The mighty works of God the King celebrated in the Psalms are wrought by the Lord of Glory in the midst of his people—he feeds the hungry, makes the lame to walk, the blind to see, the deaf to hear. He stills the roaring of the seas (Ps. 65:7), he speaks life to the dead, and gathers his remnant flock as the true Shepherd (Ezek. 34:11).

But he does not bring the judgment of God's justice, and John the Baptist sends from prison an anguished question—"Art thou he that cometh?" (Luke 7:19, ASV). Can this be the Lord whose reward is with him and his recompense before him (Isa. 40:10)?

John is blessed if he is not offended with Jesus (Luke 7:23). Christ did not come to bring the judgment but to bear it. The song of praise in the Psalms is found most often in the vow of the sufferer to render thanks to God for delivering him from the depths. Jesus Christ is the royal sufferer who cries in abandonment as he drinks the cup of wrath, but who sings in resurrection triumph as he goes up with a shout to the Father's right hand. The agonizing Savior could count all his bones as he hung on the cross, but in his triumph he will count his Father's blessings. In Psalm 22, the psalm of his agony, he utters his vow of thanksgiving: "In the midst of the congregation I will praise you" (Ps. 22:22, ESV; cited in Heb. 2:12b).

The angels sang at Christ's birth, "Glory to God in the highest," but it was the shepherds who returned from the stable, "glorifying and praising God for all the things they had heard and seen" (Luke 2:20, KJV).

The new song, God's missionary anthem, is our song. Not the holy angels but redeemed sinners sing it on planet earth, and we sing it with Jesus. Yes, Christ now sings his missionary triumph among the Gentiles: "For I say that Christ hath been made a minister of the circumcision for the truth of God, that he might confirm the promises given unto the fathers, and that the Gentiles might glorify God for his mercy; as it is written, Therefore will I give praise unto thee among the Gentiles, and sing unto thy name" (Rom. 15:8-9, ASV).

When we sing God's glory among the nations, we sing with Jesus. How Paul the apostle thrilled to hear the Gentiles with one mouth glorifying the God and Father of our Lord Jesus Christ (Rom. 15:6).

The wall of partition that shut out the Gentiles from God's altar has been broken down. The Gentiles who were afar off are now brought near, and the spiritual sacrifice of their bodies is acceptable to God (Rom. 12:1-2). The song of Moses has become the song of the Lamb, the international anthem of the redeemed who are no more strangers or aliens but fellow-citizens with the saints, joined to the commonwealth of Israel, of the household of God (Eph. 2:11-22). Only now the mountain for our festival of praise is not Sinai with its fire and smoke, or even Zion where Solomon's temple stood. Rather, it is the heavenly Zion where the saints and angels are gathered, and where Jesus is, who has sprinkled the mercy seat of heaven with his blood.

Our generation has a new perspective on this planet. We have seen its beauty, marbled with clouds, photographed from the moon. Christ's church needs a new perspective on the nations, gained not from the moon but from heaven—from that assembly where Jesus leads the song of redemption.

Stanza Two: Sing His Glorious Name!

We declare God's glory among the nations as we number his marvelous works (Ps. 96:3) and as we bless his name: "Sing to the LORD, bless His name; proclaim the good news of His salvation from day to day" (v. 2, NKJV). Praising God's works of salvation always means praising his name as Redeemer. The very name "Jesus" blesses God the Savior. He is the "Wonderful Counselor, Mighty God, Everlasting Father, Prince of Peace" (Isa. 9:6, NIV). Jesus taught us to pray, "Hallowed be thy name!" He poured out his life's blood to make that prayer our song. We declare the glory of that holy name that is made our name in Jesus Christ. Remember, you are baptized not into your own name but into God's name: the name of the Father, the Son, and the Holy Ghost.

Does the very name of God bring joy to your heart and praise to your lips? Do you remember the ten lepers sent by Jesus to show themselves to the priests at Jerusalem to be pronounced clean? Obedient, but lepers still, they set off on the long journey. What risk if they were to near the temple as lepers! But as they walked, they were healed. One of them, a Samaritan, spun about; shouting "Glory to God!" he rushed back down the rocky path to Jesus, fell headlong at his feet, and gave thanks to the Savior. Jesus said, "Were not the ten cleansed? But where are the nine?" (Luke 17:17, ASV).

"Where are the nine? Why, Jesus, they are on the road to Jerusalem. They are going where you sent them—to the priest who can pronounce them clean. Jesus, you said nothing about coming back—they are doing their duty!"

Duty? Yes, but what obedience is this that knows nothing of the joy of salvation, the praise of God's name? A sinful woman bursts unbidden into the Pharisee's dinner to wash the feet of Jesus with her tears (Matt. 26:6-13); Mary of Bethany lavishes upon Jesus the extravagant spikenard of her devotion (John 12:1-8).

Glory to God! Paul the apostle, once Saul the inquisitor, was stopped short in his persecuting rage by the glory of the Lord. He heard from his Savior's lips the name of Jesus. Ever after, he rejoiced in God's amazing grace. Reflecting on the profound depths of God's sovereign will in salvation he cried, "For of him, and through him, and to him, are all things: to whom be glory for ever. Amen" (Rom. 11:36, KJV).

Praise his name, we are called to doxological evangelism: salvation is of the Lord! Let that song die and we have nothing to sing to the nations. They don't want to hear those old patronizing songs of missionary colonialism, and they don't need our help in learning the chants of revolutionary violence. But when the people of God sing his praises, then the nations listen.

Praise his name, our God is glorious in wisdom. Kings came to learn of the wisdom of Solomon, but a greater than Solomon is here: Jesus Christ! From the cloud of glory on the mount the disciples heard the Father's command: "This is my Son, my chosen: hear ye him" (Luke 9:35, ASV). Jesus said, "Take my yoke upon you, and learn of me" (Matt. 11:29, ASV). "If ye love me, keep my commandments" (John 14:15, KJV). The words spoken by Jesus have been confirmed by those who heard (Heb. 2:3). We are to remember "the words which were spoken before by the holy prophets, and the commandment of the Lord and Saviour through your apostles" (2 Pet. 3:2, ASV).

To declare his name, we must be taught by his Word. The nations must hear of the real Jesus, the biblical Jesus. God speaks to us in his Son and commands us to listen. We cannot stand *under* the name of God and *over* the Word of God. Indeed, God's name is in his Word, for God speaks to us to reveal himself. The mystery of God's name is reflected in his Word. How soon we are beyond our depth! Yet only then can we know with Paul what it means to be lifted up with praise on the towering wave of divine wisdom.

We do not declare among the nations an empty mantra, a name that means everything and nothing. We declare the riches of God's truth, the whole counsel of God, the glory of Jesus in whom are hidden all the treasures of wisdom and knowledge (Col. 2:3).

Praise his name! We sing the glory of his power, too. God's name is hallowed in majesty in Jesus Christ our King.

Who is the King of glory? Once he rode through the hosannas and the palm branches to Jerusalem so that he might climb the hill of Calvary to die. But now he has ascended another hill. "Lift up your heads, O ye gates; even lift them up, ye everlasting doors; and the King of glory shall come in" (Ps. 24:9, KJV). The Lord mighty in battle has triumphed over the powers of darkness, and he ascends to his Father's throne. The Son, the brightness of the Father's glory, says, "All authority hath been given unto me in heaven and on earth. Go ye therefore, and make disciples of all the nations" (Matt. 28:18-19, ASV).

Christ's heavenly glory is not just a reservoir of power, an energy source to be used in discipling the nations; no, Christ's glory is the Lordship to which they are discipled. If we do not praise his name, we do not preach the gospel. We baptize into the name of the Father, Son, and Holy Ghost those who confess that Jesus Christ is *Lord*. Christ now rules over history and walks among the heavenly lampstands as the Judge of his church. Our gospel is "the gospel of the glory of Christ, who is the image of God" (2 Cor. 4:4, NKJV).

Strange as it may seem to us, we proclaim his glorious name not in the posture of conquering heroes but as ministering slaves. Sometimes, like James and John we begin to fantasize about becoming princes at Christ's right hand, or at least riding as a Rose Bowl marshall in the parade of Christ's kingdom. If that's what you have in mind, you have the right parade but the wrong place. Paul, the bondslave of Jesus Christ, pictures his ministry not as though he were riding in Christ's triumphal chariot, but as though he were a chief captive, chained to the chariot of the victorious king (2 Cor. 2:14). We carry the treasure of Christ's glorious name in earthen vessels. Pressed, perplexed, pursued, knocked down, the apostle bears in his body the dying of Jesus, knowing that he will also be raised with Jesus (4:8-14). He was made a spectacle, widely regarded as trash by the world. But what about *your* position? "I beseech you," writes Paul, "be ye imitators of me" (1 Cor. 4:16, ASV).

Yes, the name of Jesus, the King of glory, was nailed above the cross. His name is glorious in wisdom and power, and it is glorified in love. The wisdom of God is foolishness to men; the power of God is weakness to men; the love of God is an offense to men. Yet we bear before the nations God's name of love.

In the shadow of the cross, Christ's soul was troubled. He cried, "'What shall I say? Father, save me from this hour'?" (John 12:27a, KJV). That was the prayer of the afflicted psalmist, the cry of the Lord's anointed for deliverance. "But for this cause came I unto this hour" (v. 27b, KJV). Jesus came as priest and sacrifice, to give his life a ransom for many. What shall he say? What prayer but this: "Father, glorify thy name" (v. 28, KJV). Jesus, who taught his disciples to pray, "Hallowed be thy name," now prays that the Father will hallow his name at the cross. The Father in heaven replies, "I have both glorified it, and will glorify it again" (v. 28, KJV). How will the Father now glorify his name?

With the glory of legions of angels? With the glory of the cloud on the mount? No, the Father will glorify his name by lifting up his Son on Golgotha.

What glory is this? The shame of nakedness, the agony of torture, the bitter wine of mockery, the doom of abandonment. Does the elect Son glorify the Father's name when he cries, "My God, my God, why hast thou forsaken me?"

Yes, never was God's name so glorified. The eternal song of the seraphim cannot so lift it up. The devotion of the Son is fulfilled. In love to the Father he drinks the cup; in love to his own he offers his soul for sin. And the infinite love of the heart of the Father burns in the darkness. "God commendeth his love toward us, in that, while we were yet sinners, Christ died for us" (Rom. 5:8, KJV). "For God so loved the world, that he gave his only begotten Son" (John 3:16, KJV). The price that Abraham did not have to pay when Isaac was spared at the altar on Mount Moriah, that price God the Father paid when he did not spare his only begotten Son, but delivered him up for us all.

Declare among the nations the name of the God of Calvary, the glory of the love of God that sealed salvation at the cross. You may be called to sing the psalms of glory in a prison cell of affliction. Paul did that at Philippi. His bleeding back was too raw, his feet too numb in the stocks to find rest in sleep, so he found refreshment in praise: "The Lord reigns . . . the Lord is great . . . holy is he!" Is it surprising that those who glory in the cross are called to take the cross and follow Christ?

What do you seek? Is it the glory of your Lord? Lift up the Lord's great name in the praise-offering of your lips and with the thank-offering of your life. Present your bodies a living sacrifice of praise, holy, acceptable to God (Rom. 12:1).

The first question for you is not where among the nations the Lord may call you, nor even how among the nations your lips and life may declare his glory. The first question is, Have you seen the glory of the Lord? Have you heard the voice of the Son of God calling from Calvary?

Yes, you may learn of Christ the King of glory whose power will judge the warring nations, of Christ the Prophet of glory whose Word is truth for the erring nations, of Christ the Priest of glory whose sacrifice is the only salvation for the rebellious nations. But to proclaim his name among the nations, you must first bless his name in your heart.

Cry to him in repentance, call upon his name in faith, and sing the glory of Jesus Christ your Savior. Like Jehoshaphat's army of old, the church goes out to the spiritual battle singing the praises of the Lord. Jesus sang in the Upper Room with his disciples. Now he leads the praises of his people. Sing with Jesus his international anthem, the song of the Lamb! Hallelujah!

14

JESUS CHRIST AND THE
LOSTNESS OF MAN[1]

AN OLD POPULAR SONG tells it like it was:

> Don't bank down those inner fires,
> Follow out your heart's desires
> Until the day comes when they come for you;
> Make today a holiday, take tomorrow, too.
> You can't take it with you, Jack,
> And when you're gone, you can't come back.
> You're only going through!

That's an old song, well before your time. As a matter of fact, it was popular in Egypt before 1300 B.C. My version is a bit of a paraphrase. You can find a more literal translation under "A Song of the Harper" in James Pritchard's *Ancient Near Eastern Texts*.[2] For more than three millennia, men have been drinking to the idea that you only go around once, so you had better "grab for the gusto" while you can. But beneath the bravado lurks fear—the fear of death. The "morning after" is bad enough, but what of the night after? Life never escapes that shadow.

---

[1] "Jesus Christ and the Lostness of Man" by Edmund P. Clowney. Adapted from *Jesus Christ: Lord of the Universe, Hope of the World,* edited by David M. Howard. © 1974 InterVarsity Christian Fellowship/USA. Used by permission of InterVarsity Press, P.O. Box 1400, Downers Grove, IL 60515. www.ivpress.com. The message was given at InterVarsity's Urbana Conference in 1973.

[2] "A Song of the Harper," trans. John A. Wilson, in James B. Pritchard, ed., *Ancient Near Eastern Texts Relating to the Old Testament* (Princeton, N.J.: Princeton University Press, 1950), 467.

From the time of the "Song of the Harper" comes the song of another harper, full of solemn grandeur rather than trivial froth: the song of Moses the man of God, Psalm 90 in the Old Testament. Again we hear of the brevity of life: "They are as a sleep: in the morning they are like grass which groweth up. In the morning it flourisheth, and groweth up; in the evening it is cut down, and withereth" (Ps. 90:5-6, ASV).

But Moses sets the brevity of man's life in fearful contrast with God's eternity: "Even from everlasting to everlasting, thou art God. . . . A thousand years in thy sight are but as yesterday when it is past, and as a watch in the night" (vv. 2, 4, ASV).

Put against God's eternity, our living is only slow dying, and not even slow dying at that. Death's shadow flies upon us and blots out today's sunlight with tomorrow's darkness. Life is only a breath, and that breath is a sigh. The Nobel laureate playwright Samuel Beckett takes up Moses' theme in the briefest, strangest, and strongest of his plays. *Breath* is a play without a hero, without actors, without words. The stage is set with a pile of junk. As the light grows we hear a baby's birth cry, then a long inhalation, followed by a choking exhalation that ends in a death rattle. Beckett's bitter hope can offer only another birth cry as the stage sinks into darkness. "We bring our years to an end as a sigh" (v. 9, ASV). Our life-breath expires in that sigh.

Men try to come to terms with death. Fortified with arguments for immortality, Socrates drinks the hemlock with philosophic calm. Tasting the yet more bitter cup of vengefulness, a modern terrorist sows death that he may reap it. A popular Freudian philosopher warns that the fear of death is the morbid fruit of repression. Liberate the body from all repressions, he says, and it will be ready to meet death with no life unlived.[3] The opposite advice is no less ancient (or modern): Mortify the body as the prison of the soul, and hasten the absorption into the cosmic consciousness. But death's head is still visible behind the many masks we make. Even a doctor of thanatology must die.

---

[3] Norman O. Brown, *Life Against Death* (New York: Vintage, 1959), 308.

But if death is the last enemy, it does not come as a stranger. The horror of the death we do not know reaches us in the agony of the life we do know:

> I am poured out like water,
> And all of my bones are out of joint:
> My heart is like wax;
> It is melted within me.
> My strength is dried up like a potsherd;
> And my tongue cleaveth to my jaws;
> And thou hast brought me into the dust of death (Ps. 22:14-15, ASV).

The anguish of the sufferer in the psalm intensifies the sigh of frustration to a roar of agony. Man's misery is quiet despair at best. At worst it is a scream from the depths.

MAN THE REBEL

Yet all the sufferings of life and the death they foreshadow do not in themselves fill the cup of human misery. The poison in the cup of life is our guilt. Moses mourns, "Thou hast set our iniquities before thee, our secret sins in the light of thy countenance" (Ps. 90:8, ASV).

Standing beneath an empty sky, a man can strike a tragic pose as the victim of mortality. He can even pretend to be a hero of the absurd, who gives meaning to life's meaninglessness by an act of will. Albert Camus pictures Sisyphus (doomed in Tartarus) as heroically human precisely because his labor has no meaning. He toils forever to roll a rock up a hill, knowing that it will forever roll down again. "There is no fate," says Camus, "that cannot be overcome by scorn." Yet the scorn with which a man shakes his fist at the empty sky shows that the sky is not really empty. Man's sense of tragedy betrays him. Man is not a victim but a rebel. He stands before God and stands revealed for what he is—a sinner. God's holiness manifests the enormity of our crimes against our brothers. In his rebellion man can not only sanction but even sanctify his hatreds in tribal or national pride. He can brutalize his women and discard his babies. Hilarion, a traveling businessman of the year 1 B.C., writes a letter to his wife in Egypt: "If by chance you bear a child, if it is a boy, let it be, if it is a girl, cast it out."[4]

Before the living God, adultery is vile and infanticide murder. The dignity that "humanizes" man is the reflection of his likeness to God—his creation in God's image. By that image God's claim is on every man. He cannot be made a chattel or a pawn without defiance to his Maker.

When Jesus was asked whether Jews should pay taxes to Caesar, he asked to see a Roman silver coin, a denarius. One was produced from a questioner's fat purse. "Whose is this image and superscription?" asked Jesus (ASV). "Caesar's," was the reply. Jesus' retort is a double-edged sword: "Give to Caesar what is Caesar's, and to God what is God's" (Matt. 22:15-22, NIV).

We need to ponder the kingdom teaching of this Messiah who authorized Roman taxation. But even more we need to ponder the kingdom claim of the other edge of Christ's saying. Who bears the image of God? We do. What do we owe to God? Ourselves. God's image sets God's seal against all exploitation of our fellow man.

But it does much more than this. It forbids us to rob God by withholding ourselves. When the apostle Paul describes the unrighteousness of men, he begins at the beginning—with their ungodliness. They are without excuse, because "knowing God, they glorified him not as God, neither gave thanks; but became vain in their reasonings, and their senseless heart was darkened" (Rom. 1:21, ASV).

In strange ways God causes even the wrath of men to praise him (Ps. 76:10, ESV). Just as man's tragic sense witnesses to God's creation, so man's rage witnesses to God's righteousness. Try taunting some furious protester with the logic of what he claims to believe. Tell him, "Okay, so there is no God; man is a chemical accident in a random universe. What are a few thousand lives, more or less? What if a bomb suddenly reorganizes the molecules that were for the moment patterned in the form of a little girl. So what? No energy is lost."

---

[4] Quoted in C. K. Barrett, ed., *New Testament Background: Selected Documents* (New York: Macmillan, 1957), 38.

When an atheist calls you a fool or a monster, his rage for righteousness bears witness to the God he denies. We measure right and wrong by an absolute standard. We are blind not to see that the imperative of "rightness" points beyond our own desires or the desires of other men anywhere or everywhere. Only before the living God does morality find meaning. All sin is at last sin against God. The most heinous sin is the root of all other sin—rebellion against God. Because the mind of the flesh is at enmity with God (Rom. 8:7), we cannot see our sin as it is. Paul says that our understanding is darkened in the ignorance of hardened hearts (Eph. 4:18). Violence, licentiousness, greed, envy, murder—all the perversity that poisons human society springs from a deeper hate that we disguise and deny. We hate God, and we hate him because he is God: holy, just, and good.

It is the measure of our hardening that hating God is made the least of sins, perhaps even a virtue: Promethean courage against an omnipotent tyrant. When God pleads with his rebellious people in the Old Testament, he exhausts the images of broken faith to show how heinous the great sin is. Israel is a vine bearing bitter grapes to the divine vinedresser who has spared no pains in cultivation (Isaiah 5). God's people is a rebellious son turning against the father who held him in his arms and taught him to walk (Hosea 11). The nation is an adulterous wife requiting a husband's faithful love with shameless harlotry (Hosea 4).

We may be filled with rage at callous crimes of selfish violence reported in the newspaper, but we cannot comprehend the wickedness of violent rebellion against the living God. Yet our judgment is proportionate to our crime. Moses descends to one last level in his psalm of human misery. The tragedy of life is not only the vanity of our days and the sinfulness of our hearts. There is more, for the sinfulness of our hearts is open to the eyes of God: "Thou hast set our iniquities before thee, our secret sins in the light of thy countenance" (Ps. 90:8, ASV). Therefore, "we are consumed in thine anger, and in thy wrath are we troubled" (v. 7, ASV). "All our days are passed away in thy wrath" (v. 9, ASV). "Who knoweth the power of thine anger, and thy wrath according to the fear that is due unto thee?" (v. 11, ASV).

Moses' psalm has its setting in the wilderness where a generation of rebels was doomed to wander until they perished. Refusing to believe that God would give them the land of promise, they heard God's word of judgment turning them back to the desert. That word echoes in Psalm 90: "Thou turnest man to destruction; and sayest, Return, ye children of men" (v. 3, ASV).

Men are not only sinners, they are "children of wrath," subject to the righteous judgment of God. Death comes as a curse: "the wages of sin is death" (Rom. 6:23, ASV). "It is appointed unto men once to die, but after this the judgment" (Heb. 9:27, KJV).

The apostle Paul in the fifth chapter of Romans is at pains to trace the course of sin in the world to its source. Where death comes, there sin is being judged. The death-knell tolls through the genealogies of Genesis, the first book of the Bible: "and he died . . . and he died . . . and he died." Those who died were judged as sinners. Before the law had been given to Moses, before its precepts could call sin to account, men were guilty and liable to death.

At what point, then, did sin enter the world, and death through sin? Evidently in the first sin of the first man, Adam. Through one trespass death ruled over many (Rom. 5:12). Paul, of course, presses on to the parallel in salvation. As one act of sin made men guilty, caused sin to be charged against them—for all men sinned in Adam (vv. 12, 18)—so one act of righteousness brought justification and life to the new humanity in Christ.

We may need to review the apostle's reasoning in reverse. As Christians we understand that Christ was our representative who stood in our place as the Head of the new humanity. But we must also recognize the role of the first Adam in relation to the second. The guilt and judgment of Adam's transgression are shared by those who are united to Adam their head by God's creative appointment. All die in Adam because all are guilty in Adam. The sinfulness of all humanity is not a survival of the jungle: it is the result of the Fall. Man's doom stretches back to his initial rebellion and grows with his multiplied iniquity.

Before God's holiness, our ruin is complete. We are dead in trespasses and sins (Eph. 2:1). We are by nature children of wrath (v. 3). "The heart is deceitful above all things, and it is exceedingly corrupt" (Jer. 17:9, ASV). No, man is not as bad as he can be, for God restrains the hellish fury of man's corruption. But no part escapes the blight of sin. "The mind of the flesh is enmity against God, for it is not subject to the law of God, neither indeed can it be: and they that are in the flesh cannot please God" (Rom. 8:7-8, ASV).

And more—man the sinner is in bondage not only to evil but to the Evil One. He is taken captive by the snares of the devil (2 Tim. 2:26) and walks according to the prince of the powers of the air, the evil spirit that works in the sons of disobedience (Eph. 2:2). Men who were made to be sons of God have become children of the devil, doing the works of their father and doomed to share his judgment (Eph. 2:2; Matt. 25:41, 46; John 8:44).

Man's bondage to evil rolls like a subterranean river of fire through human history. In willful ignorance man fabricates his delusions and destroys himself and his world in the lusts of his idolatries (Eph. 4:18; Rom. 1:28; 6:21, 23). No man can overlook human evil; he may only add to it by condoning as pitiable that which God reveals to be damnable.

THE WRATH OF GOD

But God is not mocked. Whatever a man sows he will reap. The biblical teaching about the wrath of God is very different from the mechanical wheel of fate in Eastern religions. God cannot be a detached observer in a spiritual world of cause and effect where actions generate their own inevitable consequences. Nor is God merely a name for the process. The living God is personal: a God who reveals himself to his people as slow to anger and abundant in lovingkindness and truth (Ex. 34:6). The wrath of God is not soon kindled. God is not "vindictive" in our usual sense of the word. Yet God's wrath is the zeal of his own holiness against all sin. "Our God," warns the writer of Hebrews, "is a consuming fire" (Heb. 12:29, ASV). Not fate, not the reincarnational process of the wheel of *samsara,* but the searching knowledge of the living God judges the sinner.

Yet God does employ the fruits of our deeds to judge us. Indeed, he often makes our very sins to become our punishment. As Paul in Romans 1 describes the plunge of the heathen nations into depravity, he shows the justice of God by matching man's abandonment to sin with God's abandonment to judgment. Paul's Greek is more vivid than our translations. Men gave up the glory of the incorruptible God for idols (Rom. 1:23); God gave them up in the lusts of their hearts to uncleanness (v. 24). Men gave up the truth of God for a lie (v. 25); God gave *them* up to vile passions (v. 26). Men gave up the knowledge of God (v. 28), and God gave them up to a reprobate mind (v. 28). Even man's abandonment of natural sexual relations is judged by a divine abandonment to the chains of perversion (vv. 26-27). A man is lost as he rejects God for his own desires. His lostness is his doom as God abandons him to those desires. C. S. Lewis once said that heaven is the place where man says to God, "Thy will be done," and hell is the place where God says to man, "Thy will be done."[5] That is not the whole truth, but it catches the meaning of God's judgment as abandonment.

At last, the justice of God's judgment must be confessed by every sinner. Jean-Paul Sartre's play *No Exit* has the much-quoted line, "Hell is other people."[6] He pictures a sitting room in hell into which three strangers, one man and two women, are ushered. They are without eyelids; nothing can be changed or forgotten; and since they are already dead, murder or suicide is impossible. Given that setting, the "Hell is other people" line is easy to understand! But the climax of the play is in an earlier line. After bitter conversation has stripped away their pretensions, the "hero," Garcin, is revealed as a coward who had deserted his comrades. Inez, who has savagely torn away Garcin's lies, says, "You are your life and nothing else."[7]

"You are your life and nothing else." *No,* you cry. I am not what

---

[5] C. S. Lewis, *The Great Divorce* (New York: Macmillan, 1946), 72.
[6] Jean-Paul Sartre, *No Exit and Three Other Plays* (New York: Vintage, 1949), 47.
[7] Ibid., 45.

I have been—I am what I am going to be; I am what I meant to be. In the day of judgment, the gaze before which you will stand naked is not the lidless eyes of another sinner but the burning eyes of Almighty God. There will be no injustice, only truth; you will be revealed for what you are, and nothing else. "Yea, O Lord God, the Almighty, true and righteous are thy judgments" (Rev. 16:7, ASV). When every knee bows to God in the day of judgment, all rebellion is ended. No sinner will dispute God's sentence. The gnashing of teeth that Scripture describes on the part of those who are forever lost is no longer the gnashing of hatred and defiance, but of anguish and remorse.[8] We who still taste the possibilities of earthly life cannot imagine the meaning of existence without hope, where the guilt of past rebellion seals the abiding wrath of God. Michelangelo tried to portray the horror of the lost on the wall of the Sistine Chapel, where the damned sink down behind the altar. Yet neither Christ the Judge nor the doomed who peer out from the candle soot of the centuries are convincing figures. Far worse are the grotesque horrors of Hieronymus Bosch. No, the meaning of judgment must be approached from within, not without. The man who rejects what the Bible teaches about the last judgment should stand before God, instead of presuming to call God to account. Let him ask, before God, "What do my sins deserve?" The deepest agony of hell itself is the realization that eternal separation from God is what the sinner has demanded and deserved.

The solemn argument of Paul in Romans concludes that all men are under God's wrath because all men deserve it. The nations of the Gentiles are without excuse, for they have forsaken the God they knew. He never left himself without a witness—in the world and in their own hearts. Their very ignorance is of their own making; their false worship of their own devising; and their degrading vices their continuing delight. But when the Gentiles are condemned by self-righteous men who know the law, Paul writes a stronger condemnation. Not the hearers of the law are justified, but the doers. The man

---

[8] Henri Blocher, "La doctrine du châtiment eternel," *Ichthus* 32 (April 1973): 8.

who knows the law and disobeys is worse than the man who never knew the law. Paul's conclusion is the verdict of the psalmist: "There is none righteous, no, not one; there is none that understandeth, there is none that seeketh after God. Every mouth may be stopped, and all the world may be brought under the judgment of God" (Rom. 3:10-11, 19b, ASV).

Yes, there are mouths today that chatter on, mouths of men excusing themselves and blaming God, or excusing others to over-turn the sentence of God. The only remedy is for the man with the mouth to stand before God. If he beholds the Lord, he will cry with Job, "I have heard of thee by the hearing of the ear; but now mine eye seeth thee. Wherefore I abhor myself, and repent in dust and ashes" (Job 42:5-6, KJV).

THE GOSPEL

In describing some of the teaching of the Bible about man's lostness, I have been holding back the context in which we learn these things. To consider lostness, death, and doom by themselves, we end up splitting Bible verses in half. "The wages of sin is death"—yes, we must know that, in the sin explosion of our times—but how can we stop with "death"? "But the gift of God is eternal life through Jesus Christ our Lord" (Rom. 6:23, KJV).

The Bible reveals God's wrath in the proclamation of the gospel. Why does Paul so insist in Romans that "all have sinned, and come short of the glory of God" (3:23, KJV)? Because he wants us to know that "God hath shut up all unto disobedience, that he might have mercy upon all" (11:32, ASV). Note the connection between the rev-elation of the righteousness of God in the gospel (1:17) and the rev-elation of the wrath of God (v. 18). The wrath of God is not disclosed simply as a timeless principle of retributive righteousness. God's judgment is proclaimed as part of the news of God's purpose and work. You hear this in Paul's preaching in the book of Acts. The mes-sage of judgment calls the nations from walking in their own ways (Acts 14:16), for now God "commandeth men that they should all everywhere repent: inasmuch as he hath appointed a day in which he will judge the world in righteousness by the man whom he hath ordained; whereof he hath given assurance unto all men, in that he hath raised him from the dead" (17:30-31, ASV).

Even the appointing of a day of judgment shows God's mercy, for it means that there is time given to the nations to repent. Judgment means hope, for the day of wrath is the day of deliverance from the oppressor. Only by judgment can there be a new order, a new world of righteousness. But when a self-righteous people assumed that the day of the Lord would be all brightness for them, they were warned that they, too, must face the Judge of all the earth, who does right (Amos 5:18-20).

How, then, can the preaching of judgment bring hope to sinners? Why need they hear of a new creation delivered from groaning if they have forfeited all inheritance in it? The unimaginable answer of the gospel is that God's absolute righteousness brings salvation through the outpouring of wrath. God's good news is Jesus Christ, who comes to earth not once but twice. He will come at last to bring wrath, as the Judge of all the earth. The coming of God's kingdom in consummation power means the "revelation of the Lord Jesus from heaven with the angels of his power in flaming fire, rendering vengeance to them that know not God, and to them that obey not the gospel of our Lord Jesus; who shall suffer punishment, even eternal destruction from the face of the Lord and the glory of his might" (2 Thess. 1:7-9, ASV).

But if that were Christ's only coming, no sinner could be spared. "Who can abide the day of his coming? and who shall stand when he appeareth? for he is like a refiner's fire" (Mal. 3:2, ASV).

Even John the Baptist, Jesus' forerunner, had difficulty here. He preached the coming of the Messiah in judgment, the Messiah who would baptize with fire and hew down every tree of wickedness. When Jesus wrought miracles of healing rather than signs of wrath, when he opened the eyes of the blind rather than bringing thick darkness, when he raised the dead rather than slaying the wicked, John sent an inquiry from prison—the prison from which the

Messiah had not set him free: "Art thou he that cometh, or look we for another?" (Luke 7:19, ASV). Jesus kept John's two disciples with him while he performed more miracles of hope. "Go," he said, "and tell John the things which ye have seen and heard; the blind receive their sight, the lame walk, the lepers are cleansed, and the deaf hear, the dead are raised up, the poor have good tidings preached to them" (v. 22, ASV).

Jesus' answer reflects the prophecy of Isaiah 35:5-10, a promise of the blessings of renewal in God's kingdom of salvation. But how could blessing come without judgment? What gospel is there for the poor until their exploiters and oppressors are judged?

Jesus said to John, "Blessed is he, whosoever shall find no occasion of stumbling in me" (Luke 7:23, ASV). The answer that John awaited in faith is given to us in the gospel. Jesus came first not to wield the axe of judgment but to bear the stroke of death. Christ, the Judge who must tread the winepress of the wrath of God, Christ himself bears the wrath and drinks the cup from the Father's hand. By his blood we are saved from wrath through faith in him (Rom. 5:9). Christ was made sin for us, bore the curse for us, so that we might be made the righteousness of God in him. Only so can God be just and yet be the justifier of him who believes in Christ (3:26).

Paul preaches the revealed righteousness of God—righteousness in God's wrath against sin; righteousness as God's gift by grace— righteousness in the first and second comings of Christ. Because God's wrath struck his own Son on Calvary, it is forever past for those who are united to Jesus Christ. The gospel calls us to the cross, where wrath is swallowed up by love, where grace and justice meet.

IS GOD'S WRATH TOO SEVERE?

Is God's wrath too severe, his holiness too intense, his judgment too heavy? The measure of God's love spans the reality of his wrath. Do not tell the Father that his wrath is too great, when he must direct it against his beloved Son!

How much does the Father love his Son? The Son who was in

the bosom of the Father before the worlds were created . . . the Son, the Firstborn, of whom God says, "I will be to him a Father, and he shall be to me a Son," prays in the Garden of Gethsemane, "Father, glorify your name!" How much does the Father love the Son at Calvary as he takes the cup and is obedient to death? (Heb. 1:5).

Most of Jesus' disciples had fled. Yet his abandonment by them was not the cause of his cry. In a loud voice, he cried, "My God, my God, why have you forsaken me?" This was the cup that he must drink—the cup of the wrath of God. Never was God's judgment more severe; it was the cup of damnation that is the penalty of rebellion, blasphemy, treachery, murder—the full blood of human hatred of God. Jesus, falsely convicted by men, bore the judgment of God. He who had committed no sin took the place of those who deserved the penalty he bore. On the cross the full severity of God's wrath, the wrath of damnation, enveloped in darkness the suffering Son of God. The Father forsook his Son. He gave him up. No wonder the sun was veiled and the earth quaked. The centurion at the cross said, "Truly, this was the Son of God!"

Did the Father love the world of sinners more than he loved his own Son? The mystery of Calvary is that God so loved the world that he gave his Beloved. We can use only human language, and say that the Father never loved the Son more than when he gave him on the cross. The Father's giving was shown at Bethlehem, but fully on Golgotha. If God be for us, who can be against us? If God gave his Son for us, what will he withhold? Indeed, the gift was in God's heart before the world was made. John 3:16 does not say that God so loved his Son that he gave him the world. That is true, but the more astounding truth is that God so loved the world that he gave his Son. The measure of God's love is that for the world of lost sinners who were his enemies, the Father gave his Son, and in giving his Son, gave himself.

Yes, you have doubts; you have fears. You are sometimes bewildered. But go to the very depths of your doubts and gather them all up; take your unsolved problems, all the *whys* that come from the anguish of your heart, *whys* that grow out of major tragedies, *whys* when you do not understand. Just bring your *whys*, your questions, to God.

But come there to stay. Come there to watch Jesus Christ. Come there to listen while the God-man in his human nature cries out, "Why?" Then do not say that the Father's wrath against sin is too much.

"Who knoweth the power of thine anger?" Moses asks in Psalm 90 (v. 11, KJV). We know the answer. Jesus Christ through the power of the Father knew it, because he bore it. We must proclaim that the wrath of God is real, for God is just, and we are vile sinners. But we proclaim God's judgment in the message of the gospel. Praise God. We proclaim it in the name of Jesus.

Do not trifle with Calvary. Paul pleads,

> Or despisest thou the riches of his goodness and forbearance and longsuffering, not knowing that the goodness of God leadeth thee to repentance? But after thy hardness and impenitent heart treasurest up for thyself wrath . . . in the day when God shall judge the secrets of men, according to my gospel, by Jesus Christ (Rom. 2:4-5, 16, ASV).

No, rather, let the solemnity of God's holy wrath at Calvary open your eyes to the wonder of his love:

> Who know not Love, let him assay
> And taste that juice, which on the cross a pike
> Did set again abroach; then let him say
> If ever he did taste the like.
> Love is that liquor sweet and most divine,
> Which my God feels as blood; but I, as wine.[9]

---

[9] George Herbert, "The Agonie," in *The Works of George Herbert,* ed. F. E. Hutchinson (Oxford: Clarendon, 1941), 37.

15

HEARING IS BELIEVING:
THE LORD OF THE WORD

"SEEING IS BELIEVING." That old adage has a curious new meaning in the age of virtual reality. Digital technology can now present game players with another environment, a beginning of the "Metaverse," "a 3-D, high-bandwidth World Wide Web in which people's digital stand-ins, called avatars, interact in a giant virtual city."[1] The digital Metaverse is already under construction, and for game addicts may become more than their alternative reality.

How much did the Doom or Postal games they played condition Eric Harris and Dylan Klebold to massacre their schoolmates and themselves at Columbine High School in Littleton, Colorado? At the time, President Clinton rightly warned about the influence of such games.

Images shape and drive our culture. We are beginning to see, too, the difference it makes when God is absent from our thinking. Reality itself begins to dissolve. In its place, not merely fantasy but the interactive reality of a virtual world stands ready to take over.

The fables of the postmodern age rest on the conviction that a picture is worth a thousand words. "Seeing is believing" implies that seeing is better than hearing. In a fascinating book, *The Humiliation of the Word*,[2] Jacques Ellul relates seeing and hearing to believing. He

---

[1] Jason Fry describes the world of *Snow Crash,* a 1992 novel by Neal Stephenson, in "Novel Ideas," *Wall Street Journal,* November 16, 1998, R10. Stephenson has updated with a new novel, *Cryptonamicon* (New York: Avon, 1999).

[2] Jacques Ellul, *The Humiliation of the Word* (Grand Rapids, Mich.: Eerdmans, 1985).

finds that the proclamation of the Word has been replaced by liturgy in the high churches and by campaign spectacle in evangelical movements. He appeals to language, not merely binocular vision, as that which sets human beings apart. Language is more than the tactile signals of ants or the visual dance of bees. It is not only more complex, but different, for it is symbolic and conceptual. Ellul describes sight as immediate, locating us in spatial reality, but lacking in significance. Words, on the other hand, involve time. Meaning flows from a stream of words. Sight communicates reality; the word communicates truth.

Ellul attacks the idolatry of images, and the substitute reality they provide. Television commercials in the postmodern style flash wordless images, sometimes at the rate of two or three in a second. Such shattered images and deconstructed music dissolve all continuity into a pulsing kaleidoscope of flux. Sound bites and video flashes seem to have swept away the dull discourses of "talking heads."

We are "drowning in pictures," says Henry Grunwald, former editor of *Time* magazine.[3]

Where does that leave the preacher? David Schuringa puts the question in his doctoral dissertation, "Hearing the Word in a Visual Age."[4] His research shows the importance of the hearing of the Word in the Old Testament and the New. The ear, not the eye, appears to be the gateway for receiving revelation. He protests, however, interpreting the Second Commandment to see "the visual as the villain." He reminds us that the Bible does speak of revelation through seeing as well as through hearing. He contends that preaching must now take account of the current "epistemological shift" in the communication sciences. Meaning is now analyzed, not in terms of the intent of the sender, but in terms of the meaning given to the message by the receiver.

The shift is not so recent. For years, participants in Bible studies

---

[3] Henry Grunwald, "The Power of the Word," *Wall Street Journal,* May 19, 1999, A20. Grunwald is the author of *Twilight: Losing Sight, Gaining Insight* (New York: Knopf, 1999).

[4] H. David Schuringa, "Hearing the Word in a Visual Age: A Practical Theological Consideration of Preaching Within the Contemporary Urge to Visualization," Th.D. diss, Theologische Universiteit van de Gereformeerde Kerken, Kampen, The Netherlands, 1995.

who never heard of semiotics or hermeneutics have pronounced on "what this passage means to me." Donald Carson, in *The Gagging of God,* challenges both the prevailing theories about interpretation and the common practice of taking Scripture to mean whatever you please. Wisely, he begins not with methods of interpreting the Bible but with the God who speaks in the Bible. This must be the starting point for our understanding of the task of the preacher.[5] Schuringa, however, accepts the prevalence of the relativistic understanding of meaning on the part of the contemporary hearer, and goes on to favor the Willow Creek Church model of worship and preaching. There he finds a blending of the visual and dramatic with the preaching of the Word.[6]

The Bible does indeed speak about God's revelation in terms of seeing as well as hearing. While Ellul minimizes theophanies to defend the hearing of the Word, he, too, aims at an ultimate balance, for in Jesus Christ the full revelation of God is given.

Indeed, the living God is a jealous God who will not be worshiped through our devices. He knows the hearts of idolaters better than they do. Why, then, does he provide images of cherubim on the very cover of the ark of the covenant? Perhaps in part to show the void between them. Only the Shekinah glory may rest there. God who made man in his own image will become incarnate in the person of his Son. The throne is reserved for Jesus, the image of the invisible God (Col. 1:15), "for in Him dwells all the fullness of the Godhead bodily" (2:9, NKJV). The Father is jealous for the revelation of his Son. We cannot re-create on film the sight of Jesus. If an actor playing the role of Jesus uses his very words, those words still have power, but the face of the actor is not the face of Jesus. Everything in the expression of Jesus was revelatory, and for that revelation the Father is still jealous.

Peter, James, and John were given a foretaste of the glory of the Lord Jesus. On the Mount of Transfiguration they saw the glory of

---

[5] Donald A. Carson, *The Gagging of God: Christianity Confronts Pluralism* (Grand Rapids, Mich.: Zondervan, 1996).

[6] Schuringa's dissertation reports accurately the Reformed and biblical emphasis on the preaching and hearing of the Word of God. He provides valuable research on the issue of hearing and seeing, especially from sources in the Dutch language.

the Lord of heaven. There the climax of their seeing and hearing took place. Peter tells us in his Second Epistle: "For we did not follow cunningly devised fables when we made known to you the power and coming of our Lord Jesus Christ, but were eyewitnesses of His majesty. For He received from God the Father honor and glory when such a voice came to Him from the Excellent Glory: 'This is My beloved Son, in whom I am well pleased.' And we heard this voice which came from heaven when we were with Him on the holy mountain" (2 Pet. 1:16-18, NKJV).

Jesus had withdrawn from the crowds with his disciples, taking them far north to Caesarea Philippi. He asked them, "Who do men say that I, the Son of Man, am?" (Matt. 16:13, NKJV). When Jesus sought a better answer from them, Peter said, "You are the Christ, the Son of the living God" (v. 16, NKJV).

Peter's confession went far beyond the most flattering current opinions, and indeed it went beyond Peter. It was the Father in heaven who revealed to Peter who Jesus was and is. By revelation, Peter spoke the truth of God. Yet even Peter had to be rebuked when he would restrain Jesus from going to Jerusalem, not to conquer but to die. Peter wanted no cross for Jesus or for himself. In spite of his brash rebuke of the Lord, Peter submitted to the Lord's rebuke of him. Peter remained with Jesus, and Jesus remained with Peter. Peter and the others would follow Jesus to Jerusalem, even though he said he was going there to die. Yet Peter's daily seeing and hearing of Jesus had not of itself produced the faith that hailed Jesus as divine. That understanding came from the Father. Only afterward was Peter shown the glory of the Lord whom he had confessed. Peter did not believe because he saw the glory of Christ. He was made a witness of the glory because he believed in Christ.

The Transfiguration shows us the supreme importance of hearing the Word of the Lord. Peter, James, and John were sleepy after they had completed the long climb up Mount Hermon with Jesus.[7] There the Lord gave himself to prayer, while they nodded. The

---

[7] Since it was a high mountain, and Jesus had taken them to the region of Caesarea Philippi, Mount Hermon is presumably the place of the Transfiguration.

exploding brilliance of the light of glory roused them to awe. The light streamed, not from a cloud of glory but from the face of Jesus. That familiar face was now radiant with heavenly splendor. They saw Jesus as they had never seen him, in his glory: God the Son Incarnate. They saw him talking with Moses and Elijah, whom they somehow knew.

That was Moses and that was Elijah, not from the past, but from paradise! No wonder Peter proposed erecting three tents, first for Jesus, then for Moses and for Elijah. Heaven had come to earth. No one could doubt the coming of the kingdom, for the kingdom of heaven was present on the mountaintop. Elijah, the forerunner, was there, not just to herald the coming of the Messiah but to stand in glory beside him. Moses and Elijah had both been in the presence of the Lord on a mountaintop. Now they stood, not on Sinai or Horeb, but on Mount Hermon. Where Jesus was, there the glory of heaven had come down. Did Peter see crowds from Galilee trekking to Mount Hermon to gaze on glory? Surely sight would end all doubt.

Then the cloud that had enveloped Moses on Mount Sinai enveloped Peter, James, and John with fear. They heard, as Moses had heard, the voice speaking from the cloud. God's voice did not repeat the words of the Decalogue. There were not the ten words of command, but only one. Neither did God repeat to Elijah the promises he had heard on Mount Horeb, whispered words more fearful than the wind that flung down the rocks. No, the voice from the cloud spoke only one commandment: "This is my Son, my chosen; hear ye him" (Luke 9:35, ASV). Not *see* him in his glory, but *hear* him. Hear him as he speaks with Moses and Elijah about his exodus to be accomplished at Jerusalem.

HEAR HIM: THE PROPHET IN GLORY

Hear him, for he is the Prophet of glory. No other prophet was equal to Moses. Israel, gathered at the foot of Mount Sinai, could not bear to hear the voice of the Lord: "Let not God speak with us, lest we die!" (Ex. 20:19, NKJV). While the people stood far off, Moses went up the mountain to the thick darkness of the cloud where God was (vv. 18-21). There he entered the cloud and received the word of God (24:16-18). With Moses, God spoke "face to face, even plainly, and not in dark sayings; and he sees the form of the LORD" (Num. 12:7-8, NKJV).

Jeremiah later denounced false prophets who pretended to speak for God as though they stood in the very council of the Almighty (Jer. 23:18, 22). The true prophet speaks out of the mouth of Yahweh. That word is as sure on earth as it is in the court of heaven (v. 16).

Yet, while we may rightly find in the prophecy of Moses the validation of other prophets who were to come, his words were spoken in the singular. One Prophet will come, to whom the people must listen (Deut. 18:18).

The glory of Jesus on the mountaintop is as much greater than the glory of Moses as the Son over the house of God is greater than a servant in the house. God who spoke in the past in many and various ways has in these last days spoken finally and fully in his Son (Heb. 1:1-2). Jesus is the realization of all that the prophets promised. The message of the prophets was not only about him, it was from him, for the Spirit of Christ is the Spirit of prophecy (1 Pet. 1:11; cf. Rev. 19:10). The Son of God speaks God's last word, and *is* God's last Word. What he spoke has been confirmed by those who heard him, "God also bearing witness both with signs and wonders, with various miracles, and gifts of the Holy Spirit, according to His own will" (Heb. 2:4, NKJV).

Only One could bring to earth the whole counsel of the triune God. The Son of God, in the embrace of the Father from all eternity, has seen the Father in his own divine nature (John 6:46). He speaks and does the things that he has seen and heard with the Father. Only he can reveal the Father, just as only the Father can reveal him. If the opponents of Jesus had believed Moses' writings, they would have believed Jesus' words, for Moses wrote of him, not only in one express prophecy, but in all the Torah (5:45-47).

Moses spoke with Jesus on Mount Hermon about his offering of himself at Jerusalem. Moses well remembered the day when Israel had brought a covenant lawsuit against the Lord, accusing him of abandoning them to die of thirst in the wilderness (Ex. 17:1-7).[8] They put God on trial. At the Lord's command, Moses took the rod of judgment, summoned the elders as witnesses, and went to try the case at the Rock. There the Lord, the Second Person of the Trinity, appeared on the Rock in the glory-cloud. The Lord stood before Moses, like an accused felon in the dock, and Moses lifted his rod to strike. He dare not strike the glory in which the Lord appeared; he was told to strike the Rock, on which the Lord stood, and with which he was identified. In the songs of Moses, God is named the Rock, "a God of faithfulness and without iniquity, just and upright is he" (Deut. 32:4, ESV). In the symbol of the Rock that was his name, the Lord took the blow that Israel deserved. From the Rock flowed the water of life to the rebellious people. "The Rock that followed them," Paul wrote, "is Christ!" (1 Cor. 10:4).

Moses and Jesus spoke, not of the symbolism of the smitten Rock, but of the reality of the ultimate atonement. Jesus must go down from Mount Hermon and climb the hill of Golgotha. The Voice from the cloud said simply, "Hear him!"

Yes, his disciples must follow him. They will be eyewitnesses of what he did for us. But to know what he did, we must hear him tell us what it means. Unbelief always abandons the words of Jesus. For the hearing of faith that builds *notitia* ("information" or "truth") it substitutes the ideas of men that fabricate *error;* for the *assurance* of faith that is expressed in *assensus,* unbelief moves to the virtual reality of *illusion;* for the commitment of faith found in *fiducia* ("trust"), unbelief is enslaved to *idolatry.*

The glory of God the Son will rise infinitely higher than the highest Everest on this small planet. On the throne of his glory in the heaven of heavens, his name will be above every name. The burning seraphs will cry, "Holy, holy, holy, is the LORD of hosts," for as John tells us, Isaiah, in his temple vision, saw his glory, and spoke of him (John 12:41).

---

[8] "Meribah" (Ex. 17:7) refers to a law case. This is the use of *rîb*, the root of Meribah. "Massah," used with Meribah in verse 7, also has the juridical sense here of "trying," bringing to trial.

Yet the Lord of glory must walk down the trail of Mount Hermon with Peter, James, and John, for he must accomplish his exodus at Jerusalem.

HEAR HIM: THE PRIEST IN GLORY

Hear him, your Priest, a greater Mediator than Moses. Moses pleaded with God to spare Israel. He prayed that if the Lord in judgment destroyed the rebels, the Lord would also blot his name out of the Book of Life. But Jesus did more than share our doom; he saved us when he bore our sins in his own body on the tree.

To remember the compassion of our great High Priest, consider the experience of glory that Jesus tasted as he prayed with his face to Jerusalem (Luke 9:51). It was his own glory that he knew with the Father. That glory flooded his being and shone from his face. Surely he could return to that glory with Moses and Elijah! A chariot of fire was his to command. Need he go down to the valley again, to bear with powerless disciples who could not drive out a devil? Satan had shown him the glory of the kingdoms of the world, but on the Mount of Transfiguration, Jesus tasted the glory of the kingdom of heaven. That taste was given, not to tempt him but to strengthen him. Yes, he must go down. He could not go up with Moses and Elijah, for if he did not go down, *they* could not go up. There could be no glory for them. They spoke with Jesus about that sacrifice that was *their* hope as well as the hope of all the people of God. Jesus was strengthened in prayer, and refreshed in glory to gird him for the suffering of the damnation due to lost sinners for whom he must die. Moses and Elijah tasted a greater glory on Mount Hermon with Jesus than ever they had known. Out of Egypt God had called his Son.

No, Peter, do not attempt to set up three tabernacles, for now the true and final tabernacle has been pitched. "The Word became flesh and dwelt ["tabernacled"[9]] among us, and we have seen His glory, glory as of the only Son from the Father, full of grace and truth" (John

---

[9] "Dwelt" in the NKJV and ESV is a fair translation of *eskēnōsen*, which literally means "tented." In the context the reference is to the fulfillment of the tabernacle symbolism. The glory-cloud over the tabernacle symbolized the presence of God in his tent of dwelling.

1:14, ESV). When Moses and Elijah returned to glory, only Jesus remained with Peter, James, and John. There was none other good enough to pay the price of sin. Jesus is the Priest and Sacrifice. Once, at the end of the ages, he put away sin with the sacrifice of himself (Heb. 9:26; 10:12). Moses had sinned when he struck the Rock again to bring forth water. Only once may that blow descend on Jesus, who was made sin for us.

HEAR HIM: THE KING OF GLORY

Hear him, the King of glory. When Moses interceded with the Lord after the sin of Israel with the golden calf, he could offer no excuse, no pledge of better performance from Israel. He could only plead with the Lord to dwell in the midst of the people in his tabernacle, and to show his glory. The people had shrunk back from the glory that was reflected from the face of Moses. But on the Mount of Transfiguration, Moses did see on earth the glory of God, not a glimpse of the back of the Lord passing by the cleft of the Rock, but the full, unreflected glory of the face of the incarnate God the Son.

Elijah had triumphed over the priests of Baal on Mount Carmel when fire fell from heaven. Yet he fled in mortal weakness from the wrath of Queen Jezebel. He complained that he alone was left of all the prophets, and was about to die. The Lord in his whispered voice revealed his purposes to Elijah. He was not alone, and Elisha was already chosen. Now Elijah met the Lord, and heard his voice, the voice of the Father speaking from the cloud, and the voice of the Son, the King of glory. Jesus would be alone, for Peter, James, and John would sleep in the Garden of Gethsemane, and flee when their Lord was taken. Yet the placard above the cross witnessed to the ages: JESUS OF NAZARETH, THE KING OF THE JEWS.

HEARING IS BELIEVING

When Jesus rose from the dead, he showed himself to his disciples. They saw him, and knew him. Jesus not only appeared to Thomas but offered himself for Thomas's inspection. Let Thomas touch his wounds, and believe. Thomas did not reach out to feel Jesus' wounds. He fell at his feet, breathing, "My Lord and my God!" Jesus said, "Thomas, because you have seen Me, you have believed. Blessed are those who have not seen and yet have believed" (John 20:29, NKJV).

We have not *seen,* but we have *heard* our Lord's words. For Thomas, seeing was believing. For us, *hearing* is believing. When Jesus ascended, he did not leave an image or a portrait. The glory of Jesus that three disciples saw on a mountain before his death did not remain on earth. The visible glory of Jesus is now at the right hand of the Father. There Stephen saw him, the Lord to whom he bore witness. What remained when Jesus went to glory were the words the disciples heard and proclaimed. They heard him, and he came to them in the power of the Holy Spirit to bring to their remembrance all that he had said, and to empower them to proclaim to the nations the good news of his salvation. Jesus had not left them. The book of Acts records what Jesus continued to do and to teach through the Spirit in the days after he was received up. His Spirit came in power, and the Word of God increased and multiplied.

Writing to those in Asia Minor who had become, as Christians, strangers in their own towns, Peter spoke of the revelation of Jesus Christ. They looked forward to seeing Jesus, even as Peter looked forward to seeing him again: "Whom having not seen you love. Though now you do not see Him, yet believing, you rejoice with joy inexpressible and full of glory" (1 Pet. 1:8, NKJV). Peter had seen Jesus, and loved him. These Gentiles had never seen him, but they loved him, too. How could that be? Paul provides the answer. In the midst of his rebuke of the Galatians, he writes, "Before your very eyes Jesus Christ was clearly portrayed as crucified. . . . Did you receive the Spirit by observing the law, or by believing what you heard?" (Gal. 3:1b-2, NIV).

Paul's preaching was graphic. He preached Christ, and him crucified. But the power of his preaching was the power of the word, the power of the Spirit. The word was heard, and faith came by hearing. The portrait that Paul painted for the Galatians was not a description to make Jesus identifiable in a lineup. It was the gospel picture of what was said and done at Calvary. There, as on the Mount of Transfiguration, we must hear him.

In our world of virtual reality it is the Word of the Lord that brings realism. This is the "reality check" that dispels illusion with the sunlight of truth. In our lives and in our ministries we must hear him, Jesus Christ, the living Word.

HEAR THE LORD OF THE WORD

He who said through Moses, "Hear, O Israel: The LORD our God, the LORD is one" (Deut. 6:4, NKJV), now says to Moses and Elijah and the apostles, "Hear him."[10] Since the creation of the world, "Did any people ever hear the voice of God speaking out of the midst of the fire, as you have heard, and live?" (4:33, NKJV). But now the greater and final word of power is spoken, for the voice of the Father says, "This is my beloved Son; hear Him!" The Lord has come. The Word is himself the living God who speaks. Hear him, God the Son, through whom all things were made! "Let there be light," he says. The light that shone from his face on Mount Hermon was light that his word called into being. His is the uncreated Light shining in our darkness.

Hear him as he speaks his word of power. In a fishing boat, plunging in the gale, he stands. The disciples hear his command, "Peace, be still!" The hush of the wind and the sea terrifies them more than did the storm. "Who then is this, that even the wind and the sea obey him?" (Mark 4:41, ASV). The Lord of creation is the Lord of history (Pss. 148:7-12; 147:15-16; 46:6; 33:6, 10-11). His word struck down a blasphemous Herod and governs the powers of earth and heaven.

The deaf hear him, *"Ephphatha! Be opened!"* (Mark 7:34). The dead hear him, "Maiden, get up" (Luke 8:54). He who can say, "Lazarus, come forth!" (John 11:43), can also say, "Zacchaeus, hurry and come down, for I must stay at your house today" (Luke 19:5,

---

[10] On the importance of the "Shema," see Schuringa, "Hearing the Word in a Visual Age," 32ff.

ESV). He calls; His words are spirit and life. Like a sword they pierce the heart; his word accomplishes his commands. To a helpless sinner, he says first, "Man, your sins are forgiven you," then, "I say to you, arise, take up your bed, and go to your house" (Luke 5:20, 24, NKJV).

Jesus' word of power is therefore also a word of promise. Hear him as he invites sinners, "Come to Me, all you who labor and are heavy laden, and I will give you rest" (Matt. 11:28, NKJV). "The Son of Man has come to seek and to save that which was lost" (Luke 19:10, NKJV).

Jesus, the Lord of the Word, speaks of his saving acts. The history of his redemption is always accompanied by his revelation. The Lord declares what he will do, what he is doing, and what he has done. Hear him, the Good Shepherd! "I have come," he says, "that they may have life, and that they may have it more abundantly" (John 10:10, NKJV). Hear him, for he speaks words of pronouncement and of proclamation. In the synagogue of Nazareth he reads from the scroll of Isaiah of the Messiah's jubilee and says, "Today this Scripture is fulfilled in your hearing" (Luke 4:21, NKJV). He has come to set at liberty the oppressed, and to proclaim the year of the Lord's favor.

He gathers his disciples and teaches them his words of precept: "But I say to you, love your enemies, bless those who curse you, do good to those who hate you, and pray for those who spitefully use you and persecute you, that you may be sons of your Father in heaven" (Matt. 5:44-45, NKJV). To the rich young ruler who thought he had done all, Jesus said, "Come, take up the cross, and follow Me" (Mark 10:21, NKJV).

The Lord speaks not only in power to the waves, in judgment and warning to the Pharisees, and in so many ways to his disciples. He speaks also to his Father in prayer. "I thank You, Father, Lord of heaven and earth, that You have hidden these things from the wise and prudent and have revealed them to babes" (Matt. 11:25, NKJV). Jesus sings his Father's praise in the midst of the congregation. He makes petition for Peter that his faith should not fail. Hear him as he prays before his death, "I do not pray for these alone, but also for those who will believe in Me through their word; that they all may be one, as You, Father, are in Me, and I in You; that they also may be one in Us, that the world may believe that You sent Me" (John 17:20-21, NKJV). Hear him, too, in his cry of lament from the cross: "My God, my God, why have you forsaken me?" Hear him!

Hear him, for the Lord speaks his own name. He speaks the word of his presence. Walking on the water in the midst of the storm, he said to the terrified disciples in their foundering boat, "It is I, be not afraid!" You, as his disciple, do you hear him? It is he who says, "I carried you on eagles' wings and brought you to myself" (Ex. 19:4, NIV). He says, "Before Abraham was, I AM." He declared his covenant name to Moses from the burning bush, and he says to you, "I will not leave you as orphans; I will come to you" (John 14:18, NIV).

Would you preach the Word of the Lord? Have you heard it? Do you hear it? How may I declare to you a little of that treasure? If in the Spirit you hear one word of Jesus today, your life will be transformed. Yet you may not stay with one word. You must, day by day, hear and heed the voice of the Savior. Being a specialist in the Word does not mean that you specialize in precept only or in promise only or in pronouncement only. Preach the Word of the Lord that you have discovered afresh, or discover it for the first time. Bring from your treasure things both new and old. Drink from the fountain, feast on the banquet, fall down before the fire, draw near to the Lord.

Never forget the power of preaching the Word of the Lord. The word that grew and prevailed in the apostolic church was the word of Christ, the word of power. The gospel is the word spoken by the living, ascended Lord. What transformation the word of Christ brings to your ministry of the Word! Are you dismayed by an age that will not read, that will only look at pictures? Do you believe that Jesus Christ still speaks, and calls men and women to hear him? Tremble, preachers of the Word, for he speaks through you, if he has indeed called you and made you a proclaimer of his Word. John Murray briefly and pointedly drives home to us the words of the Apostle in Romans 10:12-21.[11] Paul who linked together the golden chain of sal-

---

[11] John Murray, *The Epistle to the Romans,* vol. 2 (Grand Rapids, Mich.: Eerdmans, 1965), 60ff.

vation in Romans 8 forged the chain of the application of the gospel in Romans 10. Here Paul speaks not of those who are called by the Lord but of those who call upon him. Who are they? Those who believe. How will they believe in him if they have not heard him? How will they hear him without a preacher? How will they preach unless they have been sent?[12]

Faith comes by hearing, not in some general sense, but by hearing Jesus Christ speak. Jesus himself is the Son who was sent by the Father, and he "speaks the words of God, for God gives the Spirit without limit" (John 3:34, NIV). He testifies to what he has seen and heard in heaven (John 3:31-32). The words that he speaks are Spirit and life (John 6:63, 68). Paul does not suppose that every believer has heard Jesus speak in the same way that he did on the Damascus road. Paul's hearing was part of his seeing the risen Lord. The Lord sent him as a chosen vessel to bear his name before Gentiles, kings, and the children of Israel. Paul as an apostle could speak of *his* gospel as that climactic revelation of the mysteries of God that enabled him to declare the word of Christ to the Gentiles as well as to the people of Israel (Eph. 3:2-12). As God's ambassador, Paul spoke for God, for God was speaking through him (2 Cor. 5:20).[13] The gospel that Paul preached was not of men, received from or taught by men, but received by revelation from Jesus Christ (Gal. 1:11-12).[14] We hear our Lord, not just in the red letters of a Bible, but in the whole revelation of the Lord, the Word.

Yet not to inspired apostles alone are the words of Christ given. Other preachers are also stewards of his word given through the apostles and prophets. You proclaim the Word of the Lord as it was

---

[12] See Schuringa's defense of the translation "hear him" as over against "hear of him" in Romans 10:14 ("Hearing the Word in a Visual Age," 53ff.).

[13] Schuringa cites F. W. Grosheide, who says that the *hōs* clause ("as though God were entreating by us" [ASV]) is not to be understood as meaning "as if" in the sense of "it appears so, but it is not so," but, rather, "as if" in the sense of "it appears as if we are doing it, but God is doing it." Thayer and G. Abbott-Smith list this verse and 2 Peter 1:3 under *hōs* with the genitive absolute as expressing the belief of the writer (or as someone's erroneous opinion). See J. H. Thayer, *Greek-English Lexicon of the New Testament*, 4th ed. (Edinburgh: T & T Clark, 1901), 681, col. 1; G. Abbott-Smith, *A Manual Greek Lexicon of the New Testament* (Edinburgh: T & T Clark, 1937), 490-491.

[14] Peter R. Jones, *La deuxième épître de Paul aux Corinthiens* (Vaux sur Seine, France: Édifac, 1992), 115.

spoken by the Lord, and confirmed by them who had heard him. We must distinguish between the revelation of the Lord by which the apostles laid the foundation of the church, and the illumination of those who built on the apostolic foundation. Not just to the apostles, but to the seventy, Jesus said, "He who hears you hears Me, he who rejects you rejects Me, and he who rejects Me rejects Him who sent Me" (Luke 10:16, NKJV; John 13:20).

The Word of the Lord is still growing and multiplying. The written Scriptures carry it, as did the Bible found in a sailor's chest by the descendants of the mutineers of the *Bounty* on their uncharted island. Persecuted Christians spread it, as they did when they were driven from Jerusalem in the days of the apostles. The Word of the Lord may be heard in small groups or in massive rallies staged by parachurch organizations, but the New Testament and especially the Pastoral Epistles remind us that the gathering of the people of God for worship remains the special place for hearing the Word of the Lord (1 Tim. 5:17; 4:11, 16; 6:3; 2 Tim. 2:14-15; 4:2; Titus 3:1).[15] It must be proclaimed in the marketplace, but it must also, and continuously, be heard in the worship of the people of God. And it must be heard from the lips of one who has been called and sent. Yes, the preaching of one called to that task is the preaching in which the words of the Lord are heard. Through your lips Jesus Christ speaks. As the Belgic Confession declares, the preaching of the Word of God is the Word of God.

If you are called to such a task, here is the Father's word to you: "This is my beloved Son. Hear him!"

---

[15] See Schuringa, "Hearing the Word in a Visual Age," 51.

General Index

SCRIPTURE INDEX